BIBLE STUDY

AUTHENTIC

DEVELOPING THE DISCIPLINES OF A SINCERE FAITH

JAMES MACDONALD

LifeWay Press®
Nashville, Tennessee

Published by LifeWay Press®
© 2013 James MacDonald
Reprinted 2014

ISBN 978-1-4158-7208-6
Item 005470535

Dewey decimal classification: 248.84
Subject headings: DISCIPLESHIP \ FAITH \ JESUS CHRIST—TEACHINGS

To order additional copies of this resource, write to LifeWay Church Resources Customer Service; One LifeWay Plaza; Nashville, TN 37234-0113; fax 615.251.5933; phone toll free 800.458.2772; order online at *www.lifeway.com;* email *orderentry@lifeway.com;* or visit the LifeWay Christian Store serving you.

Printed in the United States of America

Adult Ministry Publishing
LifeWay Church Resources
One LifeWay Plaza
Nashville, TN 37234-0152

CONTENTS

THE AUTHOR

James MacDonald has committed his life to the unapologetic proclamation of God's Word. He is the founding senior pastor of Harvest Bible Chapel, one of the fastest-growing churches in the Chicago area, reaching more than 13,000 lives each weekend. Through James's leadership and by God's grace, a church-planting ministry was formed in 2002, Harvest Bible Fellowship, which has planted more than 73 churches across North America and around the world. James also teaches on *Walk in the Word,* a daily radio broadcast committed to igniting passion in the people of God through the proclamation of truth.

Born in London, Ontario, Canada, James received his master's degree from Trinity Evangelical Divinity School in Deerfield, Illinois, and his doctorate from Phoenix Seminary. He and his wife, Kathy, have three adult children and reside in Chicago.

For more information about James and these ministries, visit *www.harvestbible.org* or *www.jamesmacdonald.com.*

Other books and Bible studies by James MacDonald:

Always True: God's Promises When Life Is Hard Bible study (LifeWay, 2011)

Always True: God's Five Promises for When Life Is Hard (Moody, 2011)

Authentic (Moody, 2013)

Downpour: He Will Come to Us like the Rain Bible study (LifeWay, 2006)

Downpour: He Will Come to Us like the Rain (B&H, 2006)

God Wrote a Book (Crossway, 2002)

Gripped by the Greatness of God Bible study (LifeWay, 2005)

Gripped by the Greatness of God (Moody, 2005)

Have the Funeral small-group study (LifeWay, 2011)

I Really Want to Change . . . So, Help Me God (Moody, 2000)

Lord, Change Me (Moody, 2012)

Lord, Change My Attitude Bible study (LifeWay, 2008)

Lord, Change My Attitude . . . Before It's Too Late (Moody, 2001)

Seven Words to Change Your Family (Moody, 2001)

When Life Is Hard Bible study (LifeWay, 2010)

When Life Is Hard (Moody, 2010)

Vertical Church (David C Cook, 2012)

Vertical Church Bible study (LifeWay, 2012)

Visit *www.lifeway.com/jamesmacdonald* for information about James MacDonald resources published by LifeWay.

INTRODUCTION

What do you think of the word *authentic?* It's a word I use to describe a life worth living. It involves people being themselves—being who God meant them to be. Unfortunately, authentic people are difficult to find. And although seeking to become an authentic person is an easy goal to set, it's harder to live out. Indeed, you may know people who spend more time talking about Christianity than actually living as Christians. You may even be such a person yourself.

That's why I've written this study. I want to help followers of Jesus develop and practice the spiritual disciplines of a sincere faith. I want us to follow in the footsteps of committed Christians across the centuries who've demonstrated that certain scriptural practices can deepen and sharpen our likeness to Christ—practices such as personal Bible study, prayer, fasting, fellowship, service, and worship.

The journey toward authenticity isn't easy, but the good news is that Jesus provides a standard for authenticity we can follow. Jesus is the real original. This is true not simply because He's our Maker and therefore qualified to tell us how to live authentically but also because He's our ultimate model. Jesus was our perfect example in every way. The disciplines of a sincere faith presented in this study are practical ways to "follow in his steps" (1 Pet. 2:21). Authentic Christians don't casually drift or roughly wander in the same direction Jesus traveled; we intentionally and purposefully follow in His steps.

Each of the disciplines we'll explore in the weeks ahead was taught and exemplified by Jesus. That's how we know they'll shape us into His likeness. These spiritual disciplines will help us live faithfully as authentic imitators of Christ. As we practice the disciplines, Jesus will work in our hearts to make us more like Him.

How to Get the Most from This Study
1. Attend each group experience.
   • Watch the DVD teaching.
   • Participate in the group discussions.
2. Complete the content in this workbook.
   • Read the daily lessons and complete the learning activities.
   • Memorize each week's suggested memory verse.
   • Be honest with God, yourself, and others about your experiences
     as you study the material and practice the disciplines.
   • Ask God to help you be obedient and open to His transformative power
     as you practice the disciplines of an authentic Christian life.

SEVEN HABITS OF HIGHLY HYPOCRITICAL PEOPLE

9-7-17

WELCOME TO THIS GROUP DISCUSSION OF
AUTHENTIC: DEVELOPING THE DISCIPLINES OF A SINCERE FAITH.

To facilitate introductions and to focus on the theme of *Authentic,* spend a few minutes talking as a group about the skills and characteristics required to become a great actor or actress. Use the following questions as the basis of your discussion.

- Which actors and actresses do you admire most? Why?

- What kinds of roles allow actors and actresses to shine best?

- What traits or habits identify a person as a mediocre performer?

What ideas or images come to mind when you hear the word *hypocrite?*

Why is it difficult to be authentic and genuine as a follower of Christ?

To prepare for the DVD segment, read aloud the following verses.

The scribes and the Pharisees sit on Moses' seat, so do and observe whatever they tell you, but not the works they do. For they preach, but do not practice. They tie up heavy burdens, hard to bear, and lay them on people's shoulders, but they themselves are not willing to move them with their finger. They do all their deeds to be seen by others. For they make their phylacteries broad and their fringes long, and they love the place of honor at feasts and the best seats in the synagogues and greetings in the marketplaces and being called rabbi by others.
Matthew 23:2-7

WATCH

COMPLETE THE VIEWER GUIDE BELOW AS YOU WATCH DVD SESSION 1.

Hypocrite: one who _pretends_ to be what he is not, assuming a position of _piety_ when in reality you are destitute of genuine faith, acting the part of being close to God when in reality your heart is very far from Him

Matthew 23

SEVEN HABITS OF HIGHLY HYPOCRITICAL PEOPLE

1. **Making salvation as** _complicated_ **as possible**

2. **Getting what I need from people even if it** _hurts_ **them**

    To be _different_ to the impact our conduct has makes us a hypocrite.

3. **Squirming my way out of any promise I don't want to** _keep_

    If you give your _word_, keep it. If you make a _promise_, keep it.

4. **Making a big deal of** _little_ **things and ignoring things of critical** _importance_

    Justice: doing what's _Right_. Mercy: going a little _Easier_ on people. Faithfulness: keep _going_.

5. **Exhibiting** _laziness_ **in all matters of the heart**

    Laziness in matters of the heart: not willing to expend the energy in the things that _Matter_ most.

    Greed: I can't get _enough_. Self-indulgence: I have no _Restraint_ in the consumption of what I have.

    We are who we are when no one can see us. That is the _true_ _you_.

6. **Looking good to others, no matter what the** _cost_

7. **Pretending to be** _better_ **than others, no matter what the evidence**

    A lifetime of unrepented hypocrisy reveals that a person has never truly been _Born_ _again_.

DISCUSS THE DVD SEGMENT WITH YOUR GROUP, USING THE QUESTIONS BELOW.

What did you like best in James's teaching? Why?

What emotions are you experiencing after hearing James teach about hypocrisy?

How do Christians often make salvation complicated? How would you explain the doctrine of salvation to someone who's never heard it?

Why is it easy for Christians to drift into hypocrisy?

Why is it damaging for Christians to practice hypocrisy in the church? In our culture?

Of the seven habits of highly hypocritical people, which have been the most damaging to you personally?

Which of the seven habits have you been forced to confront in your own heart?

Application. Before concluding this discussion, identify one of the seven habits of highly hypocritical people that you'll keep a special eye on this week. Commit to make a mental note anytime you're tempted to practice that habit and especially anytime you actually practice it. Be prepared to talk about your experiences during the next group session.

This week's Scripture memory. Matthew 15:8-9

This people honors me with their lips, but their heart is far from me; in vain do they worship me, teaching as doctrines the commandments of men.

Assignment. Read week 1 and complete the activities before the next group experience.

AN AUDIENCE OF ONE

It's been decades since I surrendered to God's call on my life, but I can still remember the way my whole world changed in those early days. All of a sudden I had new goals and new dreams. I was driven by different passions. The entire course of my life turned around. Yet even through those moments of extreme change, I also remember a deep determination to remain true to the way God made me. I didn't want to lose my offbeat sense of humor or my sometimes zany and unpredictable pursuit of fun. At the core I always wanted to be *me*.

For that reason my highest goal at age 22, fresh out of Bible college, wasn't to be a man of extreme faith or a pastor of great influence. Rather, my fervent desire was to be absolutely authentic. Of course, I wanted to be godly and biblical; I hoped to become holy and humble by God's grace. But in that process I deeply desired to remain authentic.

As I grew as a follower of Jesus, I didn't want to become fake or phony. I didn't want to be one of those guys who publicly profess spiritual intimacy with God while privately allowing their hearts to drift away from Him. And certainly I detested the idea of conforming to the pressures that other people collectively put on us as Christians (and especially as pastors) to earn their approval.

I wanted to live for an audience of One. I wanted to conform to Christ and no one else. Because I knew that anything less would turn me into something terrible and terribly destructive—something that's the direct opposite of authentic.

It would turn me into a hypocrite.

DAY 1

THE OPPOSITE OF AUTHENTICITY

Let me start this study with an unconventional caution. Namely, you might not be ready for what you'll find between these pages. In this study we'll focus on developing spiritual disciplines that, when practiced faithfully, will bring us to a more authentic walk with Christ. However, these disciplines may prove more than you're able to handle at this moment.

If you choose to take seriously the disciplines of a sincere faith, you'll notice fairly quickly that your life is no longer drifting along. You'll find a new sense of direction and purpose. That's because you'll begin taking steps toward the life that God intended rather than letting the pressures and tides of the world determine where your life is going.

But here's the warning: the most immediate reaction you'll experience when you begin a new spiritual discipline is resistance. The old you won't want to make this change. Some people in your life won't want you to alter your behavior, if for no other reason than your progress will convict them about their lack of progress. Worse, the world and the powers that control it for now won't welcome disciplined spiritual change on your part.

In other words, change is difficult. Discipline is difficult. Striving for authenticity is difficult. So you must be ready if you really plan to journey down this road.

In case we still think the point of following Jesus was to make our lives wonderful and easy, we need to remember something He said:

I have said these things to you, that in me you may have peace. In the world you will have tribulation. But take heart; I have overcome the world. John 16:33

What's your reaction to Jesus' promise that you'll have tribulation in this world?

What do you hope to experience or accomplish during this study?

Jesus didn't promise it would be easy to follow Him in this world. But the hard work of learning and practicing new spiritual disciplines will yield the reward of growing to be more like Him. If you're ready to keep reading, then let me welcome you to the next chapter in the adventure of living as a disciple of Christ. Get ready to follow in His steps.

OUR MODEL

Our goal is to become authentic followers of Jesus. As we get started, let's define *authentic* so that we'll have a common picture in mind as we explore the spiritual disciplines that can help us live a genuine, sincere faith.

What ideas or images come to mind when you hear the word *authentic*?

Here's my definition: to be authentic means to be the original article, the real thing—not a phony, knockoff, or cheap imitation. However, *authentic* doesn't necessarily mean *unique*. A craftsman may produce many authentic pieces of furniture in the same shape and style. At the core, then, something is authentic when it exactly matches what it claims to be.

We often describe something as authentic when it conforms to an original ideal or pattern and faithfully reproduces the essential features of that ideal or pattern. So we may describe a brand of hot sauce as authentic because it's blended from a secret family recipe that's been passed down through generations. The same thing can be true of jewelry, art, or even a pair of jeans.

When it comes to being authentic Christians, of course, Jesus is our original pattern. He's the ideal human being.

Read the following passages of Scripture and record what they teach about Jesus as the ideal human being.

ROMANS 5:18-21

HEBREWS 4:14-16

If Jesus is our example and the original pattern we're supposed to follow, does that mean we must be perfect like Him in order to live as authentic Christians? Thankfully, no. Notice what the apostle Paul wrote to Timothy, his protégé in the faith:

*Practice these things, immerse yourself in them, **so that all may see your progress.** Keep a close watch on yourself and on the teaching. Persist in this, for by so doing you will save both yourself and your hearers.*
1 Timothy 4:15-16, emphasis added

If you and I aim at authentic perfection, it takes only about 1.5 seconds to fall short. If we aim at genuine progress, however—if we're willing to let God keep working on us as long as it takes and no matter what it takes—things will happen.

> **Describe a time when you felt that you were making progress in your spiritual growth. What spurred that growth?**

Unfortunately, there are many obstacles that can impede our progress on the journey toward authenticity. And none are bigger or more destructive than hypocrisy.

BEWARE THE MASK

I want to be authentic! Experience tells me that we can't start examining authenticity until we've confronted hypocrisy. We won't take seriously the practices of a sincere faith until we recognize the danger of being artificial.

Believe me, there's a lot of pretense out there. All of us know people who wear masks, acting as though they're something they're not. And if we aren't careful, hypocrisy is an easy act to fall into ourselves.

> **What ideas or images come to mind when you hear the word *hypocrisy*?**

> **When have you recently been affected by insincerity or hypocrisy?**

It would be massively hypocritical and truly inauthentic of me to race into this subject without stopping to disclose my own battles with hypocrisy. Although, by God's grace, there's nothing behind the curtain that would make you want to throw this book into the fireplace, I've had seasons in my life when my public walk outpaced my private walk, leading to relational fallout and bitter tears.

What seasons of your life have been marked by hypocrisy?

What were some of the consequences of that hypocrisy?

Nothing will shred your soul faster than the acceptance of hypocrisy, so we're going to deal with it head-on this week. In fact, we're going to explore seven habits of highly hypocritical people—all of which are found in Jesus' confrontation with a group of Pharisees in Matthew 23.

Read Matthew 23:1-12. What behaviors did Jesus point out as hypocritical?

What does it mean for a person to humble himself (see v. 12)?

Do these verses make you a little uncomfortable? They should. Jesus didn't mince words when it came to hypocrisy. He went hard after it, and so will we this week!

DAY 2

HYPOCRISY AND SALVATION

Nobody likes receiving bad news. Our culture promotes a lot of different techniques to soften the impact of negative news. For example, we might ask someone to sit down before delivering the news or encourage someone to look for the silver lining. But at the end of the day, bad news will always be bad news. And bad news stinks.

What do you dislike most about receiving bad news? What do you dislike most about delivering bad news?

Today we're diving deeper into Matthew 23, where Jesus delivered some seriously bad news to the Pharisees and other religious leaders of His day.

WOE TO YOU

Jesus got straight to the point in verse 13: "Woe to you, scribes and Pharisees, hypocrites!" Can you imagine what it would be like to hear these words directed at you from the mouth of Jesus? Those religious leaders must have been offended, especially if they grasped the severity of the word Jesus used.

What do you think Jesus meant by the word *woe*?

Read Matthew 23:13-29. What were the Pharisees doing that caused Jesus to confront them?

Jesus repeated the word *woe* seven times in verses 13-29. In our day we use it to express suffering or trouble. But that term in the original Greek is *ouai,* which in Jesus' day wasn't so much a word of sorrow or calamity but a heart cry of anger, pain, and denunciation. It was an expression of grief and profound dissatisfaction. Spoken by Jesus, it was a divine proclamation of judgment. He pronounced God's verdict on the hypocrites and pointed to their future sentencing in eternity.

The word *hypocrite* is such a powerful term that instead of trying to translate it, we've simply transferred it from Greek *(hupocrites)* into English. The expression originated from theatrical practices in ancient times, when actors wore masks rather than makeup to hide their true identities. In fact, the word *hypocrite* was originally a compliment for actors with theatrical skills. Over time the term changed and became a label for people who portray themselves as something they aren't.

Christians are hypocrites when they assume a position of false piety, making themselves out to be mature believers when in reality they're destitute of genuine faith. Hypocrites act the part of being close to God when their hearts are very far from Him.

> Read the following verses and record what they contribute to your understanding of what it means to be a hypocrite.
>
> MATTHEW 6:1-4
>
> MATTHEW 7:1-5
>
> 1 JOHN 4:20-21

Jesus said of the Pharisees, "This people honors me with their lips, but their heart is far from me" (Matt. 15:8). This phrase describes the general attitude behind what I call the seven habits of highly hypocritical people.

Let me warn you that no one is entirely exempt from hypocrisy. In fact, you should be concerned if you read the lessons this week without experiencing a moment of conviction about your personal shortcomings. We've all been hypocrites or liars to one extent or another—just one piece of evidence confirming that we're fallen human beings who desperately need God's forgiveness and grace. So as we go through these characteristics, I encourage you to evaluate yourself by asking, *Am I like that? Do I do that?*

HABIT 1: HYPOCRITES MAKE SALVATION AS COMPLICATED AS POSSIBLE

Here's Jesus' first pronouncement of woe to the religious leaders of His day:

Woe to you, scribes and Pharisees, hypocrites! For you shut the kingdom of heaven in people's faces. For you neither enter yourselves nor allow those who would enter to go in. Matthew 23:13

What emotions did you experience when you read these words? Why?

The expression "the kingdom of heaven" is a reference to salvation. Jesus was talking about gaining entrance into God's family, and He criticized the Pharisees for making things more complicated than they needed to be. The Pharisees had rejected the Messiah as the way to God, and they "shut the kingdom of heaven in people's faces" by misleading them about what it took to please God. Instead of accepting God's free offer of salvation, the religious leaders had erected barriers to the kingdom by requiring adherence to thousands of man-made religious laws.

Salvation is simple, but there's nothing easy about it. Salvation came at a great cost to Jesus as He sacrificed Himself on the cross for our sins. And it's not easy for us to give up control of our lives in submission to Christ in order to accept His forgiveness. But salvation isn't complicated in terms of intellectual understanding.

> **Read the following passages of Scripture and record what they teach about the concept of salvation.**
>
> **JOHN 3:16-17**
>
> **ROMANS 10:9-10**
>
> **EPHESIANS 2:8-9**
>
> **How do some churches or groups today try to make salvation complicated?**

Hypocrites make salvation complicated by leading people into religious systems instead of a personal relationship with Jesus Christ. Why? So that they can feel superior and be treated as the guardians of God's kingdom who have special knowledge or spiritual standing: "You've got to do these 15 things." "You've got to follow these steps to enlightenment." "You've got to manifest this particular spiritual fruit to prove you're saved." "You've got to practice these seven sacraments perfectly, or you can't be saved. And if the system fails, it's your fault. So you'd better come to church and keep all of the rules."

Talk about shutting the kingdom in someone's face!

When have you been guilty of making the message of salvation more complicated than it needs to be?

I love a testimony that reveals people who want to share the joy of salvation with others. All it takes is one person reaching out to another person in love. The invitation can be as simple and direct as "I want to pray with you to receive Christ as Savior and Lord." That's what sincere people do: love and care for those who are lost and hurting without making it a religious, complicated, 87-step process to receive what God freely offers.

What a tragedy when people accept Christ simply and then gradually come to view the gospel as something so complex that they can't pass it on effectively. It's as if they think, *I got saved, but I can't possibly tell you how to get saved. It's so complicated that I might get it wrong.*

What obstacles prevent or hinder you from sharing the gospel more often?

How would you express the core message of the gospel in a single sentence?

As we continue to explore Matthew 23 in the days to come, remember that the Pharisees chastised by Jesus were the most religious people of their day. They were the Bible-carrying believers; they were the spiritual role models. So if we're serious about God's Word and if we aspire to be spiritual role models, then we're possibly contemporary parallels to the Pharisees. Therefore, we must regularly check ourselves against the standard Jesus used to invite others into His kingdom, unhindered by legalistic requirements of our own invention.

May God help us keep the message of Christ's love and forgiveness simple and available to everyone. Anything else is hypocrisy.

DAY 3

USING PEOPLE AND BREAKING PROMISES

There are lots of different jobs and tasks that need to be tackled in today's world, and for that reason we've designed lots of tools that help us tackle them. We've got wrenches and drills and measuring tapes for building projects. We've got pans and measuring cups and ovens for baking projects. We've got paint and rulers and color wheels for design projects. And on and on it goes.

There's nothing wrong with using tools to help us achieve our desires. In a way, tools are designed to be exploited for our gain.

People are different. We're created in the image of God (see Gen. 1:26-27). Therefore, it's a terrible shame when people are used inappropriately—when people are beaten down or exploited for the benefit of others. People aren't tools.

When have you been used or exploited by others?

What emotions did you experience during and after these encounters?

As we continue our exploration of Matthew 23, we feel Jesus' righteous rage at the way His people were being used and abused at the hands of hypocrites.

HABIT 2: HYPOCRITES TAKE WHAT THEY NEED FROM OTHERS EVEN IF IT HURTS THEM

Look at Jesus' second pronouncement against the religious leaders of His day:

Woe to you, scribes and Pharisees, hypocrites! For you devour widows' houses and for a pretense you make long prayers; therefore you will receive the greater condemnation. Matthew 23:14, text note

Read the following passages and record ways they enhance your understanding of Jesus' words in Matthew 23:14.

PSALM 68:4-6

JAMES 1:27

Widows in Jesus' day had many needs and few resources. We're challenged throughout Scripture to care for the powerless in the church, including widows and orphans. We're commanded to love them and help them. We're responsible to care for everyone who has many hardships and few resources.

Hypocrites do the opposite. These religious men saw someone in poverty but arrogantly devoured the little they had: "Even though you don't have much, God wants me to have your meager supply for myself. So we're going to require more offerings and sacrifices and pretend they were God's idea." It's the idea of personal gain even if it hurts others.

Yet there was more to this highly hypocritical habit:

Woe to you, scribes and Pharisees, hypocrites! For you travel across sea and land to make a single proselyte, and when he becomes a proselyte, you make him twice as much a child of hell as yourselves. Matthew 23:15

In Jesus' day the scribes and Pharisees made great efforts to convert Gentiles to Judaism. But after doing so, the Jewish leaders indoctrinated the new converts in a false system of legalistic religious works. Without experiencing a personal relationship with God through Christ, these converts inevitably became hypocrites like their religious leaders.

The simple truth is that hypocrites hurt people; they don't help them. They do damage in the name of God—an idea that should be anathema to the heart of a Christian.

What actions have you seen Christians take that hurt others?

I wish I could say that I've never met people like that, but I certainly have: ruthless in the marketplace, vindictive and petty in the neighborhood, and self-serving and demanding at church. Take. Take. Take. I'm always amazed by Christians who claim to love the Lord but leave a trail of hurting people in their wake and never seem to give a second thought about the damage they've caused.

Have you injured others and callously turned away? Have you knowingly done things to wound people and then come to church and participated without hesitation? Do your children carry scars from your hypocrisy? Are there people where you work whom you hate? *That* is hypocrisy. And it can't exist unchallenged in a New Testament church or in the life of an authentic disciple of Jesus.

> **Which of the previous questions, if any, cause you to feel convicted? What steps can you take to repair the damage you've caused by exploiting or misleading others?**

Jesus condemned not only the religious leaders' hypocrisy but also the fact that they led others astray: "You make him twice as much a son of hell as yourselves" (v. 15). If there's a persistent pattern of hypocrisy in our lives that hurts others and detracts from the worship of Jesus, it raises legitimate questions about the reality of our faith. With humility we must confront any personal hypocrisy, recognizing and seeking God's grace. Yes, God loves us despite our hypocrisy, but He never wants us to be comfortable with it!

HABIT 3: HYPOCRITES SQUIRM OUT OF PROMISES THEY DON'T WANT TO KEEP

Jesus continued to work through His docket of denunciation against the Pharisees in Matthew 23:16-17:

Woe to you, blind guides, who say, "If anyone swears by the temple, it is nothing, but if anyone swears by the gold of the temple, he is bound by his oath." You blind fools! For which is greater, the gold or the temple that has made the gold sacred?

Apparently, the Pharisees had a fingers-crossed-behind-your-back clause in their commitments. The religious leaders put on a show of making vows and paying tithes. They'd say, "I swear by the temple that I'll do this." And then someone would say, "Hey! You swore by the temple you'd do it, but you're not doing it!" The Pharisees would respond, "Ah, but I didn't swear by the *gold* in the temple!"

What? Doesn't that sound ridiculous? Yet Jesus addressed a similar pattern of behavior in verses 18-19. The religious leaders made vows but then squirmed away from a promise if they swore something on the altar rather than the *gift* on the altar; that's how twisted their minds had become.

Basically, the Pharisees were splitting hairs and using any methods they could find to avoid keeping their word whenever it wasn't convenient or beneficial for them to do so. They claimed before the people to be sincere in taking oaths, but in reality they never intended to keep their promises. Then they expected to be released from promises based on hidden technicalities. Sound familiar?

In what ways do people use hidden clauses and technicalities to avoid responsibility in today's society? In the church?

Here's the scary part: I've made some big promises in my life. One Savior for life. One wife for life. One church for life if God allows. I'm guessing you've made some pretty big promises as well.

What are some major commitments you've made during your life?

What are some promises to God or others you've made in recent months?

Trust me; your commitments will get tested—if they haven't been tested already. There will be times when it will be a lot easier to break your word and go in a different direction. As Christians, we must recognize that giving our word on something always comes with a cost. Ecclesiastes 5:4-5 says:

When you vow a vow to God, do not delay paying it, for he has no pleasure in fools. Pay what you vow. It is better that you should not vow than that you should vow and not pay.

Pay what you vow to pay. Do what you say you'll do. If you make a commitment to do something for the kingdom of God, follow through on it. Deliver on what you promise or else don't make a promise. That's what sincere, honest people do. That's what followers of Jesus should always do. Hypocrites, though, squirm out of any promise they don't want to keep.

DAY 4

MOUNTAINS AND MOLEHILLS

As someone who aspires to be a lifelong learner, I try to stay as informed as I can about history—about the foundational moments and events that forever changed the course of cultures, nations, and the church. I'm talking about events like the signing of the Declaration of Independence, Luther's posting his 95 Theses, the assassination of Julius Caesar, and so on. I'd love to go back in time and be a fly on the wall during those hugely significant moments. Wouldn't you?

I don't think Jesus' confrontation of the Pharisees in Matthew 23 was the most significant thing He did, but I'd still like to have been there. I'd love to have seen the faces of the religious leaders as Jesus, revealing a glimpse of His true authority, crushed their hypocrisy. I'd love to have seen the reactions of the people on the street as they witnessed this conversation and heard what God really thinks about hypocrites who claim to serve Him but actually serve themselves.

We can't go back and witness that scene, unfortunately. But we can relive it as we continue our study of the seven habits of highly hypocritical people.

HABIT 4: HYPOCRITES MAKE A BIG DEAL ABOUT LITTLE THINGS WHILE IGNORING WHAT'S IMPORTANT

Here's how Jesus unveiled His fourth woe to the Pharisees:

Woe to you, scribes and Pharisees, hypocrites! For you tithe mint and dill and cumin, and have neglected the weightier matters of the law: justice and mercy and faithfulness. These you ought to have done, without neglecting the others. You blind guides, straining out a gnat and swallowing a camel!
Matthew 23:23-24

> **Read Micah 6:8. How does that verse connect with Jesus' rebuke of the Pharisees?**

Tithing is the biblical principle of giving 10 percent of your income off the top to God. In the Old Testament, of course, giving mostly involved commodities instead of money. If you had an apple orchard, you brought a tenth of those apples to the temple to use in worship and to support the priests. If you had livestock, you contributed a tenth of the increase. Even so, the Bible never prescribed anything in regard to the little garden out behind your house where you raised herbs for cooking.

Enter the Pharisees. These guys were so legalistic that they'd hold a little sprig of parsley and say, "One leaf for God, nine leaves for me; one leaf for God, nine leaves for me. I'm so godly!" In the law God never asked for that level of measuring the tithe. That's something the legalistic Pharisees added to God's law.

Why is it so tempting for Christians to become legalistic about obeying specific rules?

But microtithing wasn't the real problem for Jesus. He spoke against the Pharisees because they were so energetic about little things like herbs, yet they ignored matters of massive importance—things like justice, mercy, and faithfulness.

I love the emphasis on those three principles. When Christ said "justice," He was talking about doing what's right. You may well be facing a big decision this week. Do you know what you should do? Let me tell you: if you've prayed about it, go ahead and do what's right. Do what's right! Right action will always take you to a good place.

Jesus also emphasized mercy. That means going a little easier on people. Instead of shoving judgment down their throats, make room for others to experience conviction, repentance, and reconciliation. James 2:13 says, "Judgment is without mercy to one who has shown no mercy. Mercy triumphs over judgment." Be merciful.

The last principle Jesus emphasized was faithfulness. Just keep going. Don't give up. Don't let anything stop you. Be faithful to continue in your walk with God.

Jesus said God didn't care that the Pharisees were tithing the little herbs. Justice, mercy, faithfulness—that's what God cares about!

Do you find it easier to focus on justice, mercy, or faithfulness? Why?

In what areas of life have you made minor religious rules more important than they should be?

Following Jesus is all about justice, mercy, and faithfulness. Those are the big-ticket items for Christians. Those are the concepts that should capture our attention.

HABIT 5: HYPOCRITES ARE LAZY IN ALL MATTERS OF THE HEART

Jesus' next pronouncement of judgment on the Pharisees was especially devastating:

Woe to you, scribes and Pharisees, hypocrites! For you clean the outside of the cup and the plate, but inside they are full of greed and self-indulgence. You blind Pharisee! First clean the inside of the cup and the plate, that the outside also may be clean. Matthew 23:25-26

Notice the word picture Jesus used. Imagine a guy holding a cup in his hands, ready to take a big drink. The cup looks lovely on the outside—it's polished and shining with gold and jewels—but the inside of the cup is filthy; it's lined with a layer of mildewy scuzz. Imagine that guy filling his cup with water and then chugging it down, delighting in the *appearance* of the container but totally careless about imbibing the filth it holds.

Jesus didn't mince words in describing what's inside the beautiful cup: "Inside they are full of greed and self-indulgence" (v. 25). That's a very bad combination. Greed is "I can't get enough." Self-indulgence is "I have no restraint in the consumption of what I have." That's how Jesus assessed the Pharisees' hearts. And the same words He used are a great description of our society today.

How do you see greed and self-indulgence lifted up in today's society?

In what ways do you struggle with greed and self-indulgence?

The big question is why. Why would someone be willing to drink from a cup that's filthy and disgusting on the inside? Jesus' answer was laziness: "You blind Pharisee! First clean the inside of the cup and the plate, that the outside also may be clean" (v. 26).

The Pharisees demonstrated laziness in all matters of the heart—in anything having to do with their personal walks with God. Jesus exposed the laziness of hypocrisy in their spiritual lives. He exposed the unwillingness of hypocrites to expend energy in loving God. Although the Pharisees took great pains to beautify the exterior of their lives through outer religious works, they were lazy in dealing with the internal filth of sin in their lives. Too lethargic to work? They stole. Too lazy to discipline themselves? They fed on what they stole without restraint. They weren't willing to expend any effort on unseen spiritual pursuits.

We're most truly who we are when no one is watching us. When we think someone will see what we're doing, when we know others will know, we optimize the appearance of what we do. But the way we behave when nobody else is watching and no one will know what we do—that's who we truly are.

Do you make an effort to behave differently when you know people are watching? Explain.

Are you lazy when it comes to the deep condition of your soul and your faith? In what ways?

If you're feeling stung, that's OK. Jesus' words in these verses were meant as a rebuke, not just to the Pharisees but to all hypocrites, including you and me. If you've identified areas of hypocrisy in your spiritual life, you shouldn't be satisfied with your condition.

In fact, if you don't feel convicted after reading Jesus' words, that's dangerous. If you're thinking, *Why do I have to deal with this stuff when I was just getting ready to watch the game?* that's a bad sign. That's hypocritical apathy—exhibiting laziness in matters of the heart. That's being stuck and not caring enough to admit that you just don't want to do the hard work of nurturing your relationship with God. What a tragedy to display hypocrisy with Jesus' word *woe* ringing in our ears.

DAY 5

MAINTAINING APPEARANCES

Are you still with me after four days of focusing on hypocrisy? I hope so. We've been crawling through the muck and mire of a difficult subject, but there's light at the end of the tunnel now. We're almost out!

Take a moment to prepare your heart and mind. Then join me in plowing through the final two habits of highly hypocritical people.

HABIT 6: HYPOCRITES LOOK GOOD TO OTHERS, NO MATTER THE COST

If you stand on the Mount of Olives in Israel, the valley between you and the city of Jerusalem is a cemetery—a wall-to-wall burial ground. There are graves as far as the eye can see. And every year before Passover, people used to clean the grave covers stained by weather or dirtied by birds and then whitewash everything. It was said that Jerusalem gleamed in the sunlight during the weeks before the festival.

Keep that image in mind as you read these words from Jesus:

Woe to you, scribes and Pharisees, hypocrites! For you are like whitewashed tombs, which outwardly appear beautiful, but within are full of dead people's bones and all uncleanness. So you also outwardly appear righteous to others, but within you are full of hypocrisy and lawlessness. Matthew 23:27-28

Hypocrites care deeply about how they appear to others. They desire to build up their reputations and their respectability even as they rot on the inside because of unrepented sin. This offensive habit takes hypocrisy to a new level: "I'm going to look good. I'm going to wear and flaunt an attractive façade. I don't care what it costs."

Why do we care so much about what others think of us?

What steps do you take to enhance your reputation with friends and family?

By comparing the Pharisees to whitewashed tombs (see v. 27), Jesus was using a very strong image to condemn the Pharisees' hypocrisy. His listeners knew that according to the law, anyone who came in contact with a dead body was unclean (see Num. 19:11). So Jesus was saying underneath the Pharisees' polished spiritual practices lay hearts of uncleanness and wickedness.

If you don't think Jesus' words apply to Christians today—that is, if you don't think they apply to you—think again. How many times do you come to church in your best outfit but without a shred of spiritual readiness inside? You'd probably never think of arriving at church with bedhead and wrinkled clothes, yet how often do you enter the sanctuary without having devoted a moment to prayerfully preparing your heart? Without spending any time in God's Word cultivating a teachable spirit?

What bothers you more—hearing that your children misbehaved in Sunday School or knowing that God sees your disobedience? Arriving at church with your hair out of place or your heart unprepared? What upsets you most—a spot on your shirt, a stain on your dress, or a lump of unrepentance in your heart?

What emotions did you experience when you read the previous questions?

What spiritual preparation would be appropriate before believers come to church?

Being content with an external shell that misleads others into thinking all is well on the inside is an attitude that God will not leave untroubled. So are you troubled?

HABIT 7: HYPOCRITES PRETEND TO BE BETTER THAN OTHERS
Jesus ended His list of woes to the religious leaders of His day:

Woe to you, scribes and Pharisees, hypocrites! For you build the tombs of the prophets and decorate the monuments of the righteous, saying, "If we had lived in the days of our fathers, we would not have taken part with them in shedding the blood of the prophets." Thus you witness against yourselves that you are sons of those who murdered the prophets. Matthew 23:29-31

What do you find most interesting in these verses? Why?

The people of Jesus' day greatly revered the ancient prophets from the Old Testament such as Isaiah, Jeremiah, Ezekiel, Daniel, and many more. This was strange, since many of those prophets had been murdered by the ancient Israelites. Stranger still, the religious leaders of Jesus' day went so far as to decorate the tombs of the prophets who'd been killed for speaking God's truth, claiming, "If we'd lived in their day, we wouldn't have killed the prophets. We're better than our ancestors."

How often do you find yourself saying you could do something better than another person?

What standards do you typically use when comparing yourself with others?

Jesus recognized the Pharisees' claim as another false show of piety. What followed was one of the hardest statements in all of Christ's teaching:

Fill up, then, the measure of your fathers. You serpents, you brood of vipers, how are you to escape being sentenced to hell? Therefore I send you prophets and wise men and scribes, some of whom you will kill and crucify, and some you will flog in your synagogues and persecute from town to town, so that on you may come all the righteous blood shed on earth, from the blood of righteous Abel to the blood of Zechariah the son of Barachiah, whom you murdered between the sanctuary and the altar. Matthew 23:32-35

The Pharisees and other religious leaders claimed not only to be righteous but also to be more righteous than their ancestors. They were blind to the sinfulness of their hearts, but Jesus saw it clearly. He knew these were the same people who were just days away from murdering Him on a cross. By telling them to "fill up … the measure of your fathers" (v. 32), Jesus was saying their future actions would prove that they were just as evil as their forefathers.

Hear this: a lifetime of unrepentant hypocrisy reveals that a person has never truly been born again.

What's your reaction to the previous statement? Why?

As you read these words, if God's Spirit is provoking conviction in your heart about areas of your life that need to improve or change, that's a good sign. There's hope for you! But if all you're thinking about is what others need to learn and what a fine Christian you are, I fear for you. I pray that you'll rethink the implications of these words from Jesus.

Verse 36 should give us pause as well: "Truly, I say to you, all these things will come upon this generation." Jesus was speaking directly to His audience at that time, but much of what He said applies today. What would He say to this generation about the seven habits of hypocritical people? Are we like that? Do we do that?

As you begin this journey through the disciplines of a sincere faith, I pray that you'll deeply acknowledge any tendency toward hypocrisy in your heart. I pray that you'll ask God to prepare your heart for a more authentic walk of faith.

How have you been convicted during this week's study of hypocrisy?

What steps will you take in the coming weeks to repent of hypocrisy and seek an authentic spiritual life?

To finish up this exploration of hypocrisy, I want to make sure we don't miss the heart of Jesus behind His words to the Pharisees. If at any time during this study you've imagined Jesus spitting out, "You hypocrite!" and then turning His back on you, you've got it wrong. You've missed the heart of what Jesus said to the Pharisees—and to us.

Look at Jesus' cry of anguish near the end of His proclamations against the hypocrisy of the religious leaders:

O Jerusalem, Jerusalem, the city that kills the prophets and stones those who are sent to it! How often would I have gathered your children together as a hen gathers her brood under her wings, and you were not willing! Matthew 23:37

What emotions do you detect in these words from Jesus?

What obstacles prevent us from seeing hypocrisy in our lives?

Jesus doesn't want to bash us over the head with our hypocrisy. He doesn't want to throw it in our faces and make us feel guilty or ashamed. When we recognize our hypocrisy, He wants us to turn away from it, and He wants us to turn toward Him.

Sadly, many people hear God's invitation to abandon their hypocrisy, yet they refuse to answer His call. I pray that won't be true of you or me, because stubbornness of the heart is a terminal sickness. There's no solution for that condition apart from repentance and God's work of grace to break our hearts.

THE DISCIPLINE OF PERSONAL BIBLE STUDY

WELCOME BACK TO THIS GROUP DISCUSSION OF
AUTHENTIC: DEVELOPING THE DISCIPLINES OF A SINCERE FAITH.

The previous session's application activity challenged you to be alert to a specific hypocritical habit through the week. If you're comfortable, talk about your experiences with that habit.

Describe what you liked best about the lessons in week 1. What questions do you have?

Once we've identified an area of hypocrisy in our lives, how can we move forward toward authenticity?

What ideas or images come to mind when you hear the phrase *Bible study?* Why?

To prepare for the DVD segment, read aloud the following verses.

Blessed is the man
who walks not in the counsel of the wicked,
nor stands in the way of sinners,
nor sits in the seat of scoffers;
but his delight is in the law of the LORD,
and on his law he meditates day and night.
He is like a tree
planted by streams of water
that yields its fruit in its season,
and its leaf does not wither.
In all that he does, he prospers.
Psalm 1:1-3

WATCH

COMPLETE THE VIEWER GUIDE BELOW AS YOU WATCH DVD SESSION 2.

THE DISCIPLINE OF PERSONAL BIBLE STUDY

1. _pick_ **it up.**

   The Bible is _beyond_ any other book.

   God's Word _transforms_ you.

   God's Word gives you _wisdom_.

   God's Word brings you _joy_.

   Precepts: divine _principles_, rulings, prescriptions, pronouncements, charges

   God's Word dispels the _darkness_.

   God's commands are _clear_.

   The commands of the Lord are so crystal clear that they bring _light_ to the darkness in every human heart.

   Fear of the Lord: the attitude of heart that seeks to be in a right _relationship_ with the fear source

   God's Word adds _stability_. God's Word promises _justice_.

   Rules: rulings, _judgements_, verdicts, pronouncements, consequences, decisive actions

2. _Size_ **it up.**

   God's Word is a _sword_.   God's Word is a _meat_.

   God's Word is a _hammer_.   God's Word is a _light_.

   God's Word is _seed_.   God's Word is _mirror_.

   God's Word is a _milk_.   God's Word is a _fire_.

3. _Eat_ **it up.**

   Read it. _Question_ it.

   Is there an _Example_ for me to follow?

   Is there a _sin_ for me to confess?

   Is there a _truth_ for me to understand?

   Is there a _Comfort_ for me to embrace?

   Plan it. _Pray_ it. _Share_ it.

DISCUSS THE DVD SEGMENT WITH YOUR GROUP, USING THE QUESTIONS BELOW.

What did you like best in James's teaching? Why?

What are the biggest differences between hypocrisy and authenticity?

To what degree are you satisfied with your current experiences in studying God's Word?

How have you been personally affected by picking up God's Word?

Respond to James's statement: "The greatest student of Scripture in our church has not begun to plumb the depths of what's in God's Word. It can satisfy the greatest minds for a lifetime and beyond."

What changes do you experience as a follower of Jesus when you begin to drift away from the Scriptures?

What practices help you internalize and apply the truths you encounter in the Bible?

Application. Commit to take notes each time you study God's Word throughout the week. Whenever you encounter a passage of Scripture, write down your answers to these three questions:

1. What does the text say?

2. What does the text mean?

3. How does the text apply to my life?

This week's Scripture memory. Psalm 19:14

*Let the words of my mouth and the meditation of my heart
be acceptable in your sight,
O LORD, my rock and my redeemer.*

Assignment. Read week 2 and complete the activities before the next group experience.

WASH IT OFF

I'm a full-time pastor, which means I need to stay pretty clean most of the time—and I mean clean in the physical sense. Of course, I also need to stay spiritually clean, but hopefully that's a given for all followers of Jesus. Because I spend a lot of my time in the company of other people, it's important that I don't look or smell offensive.

Even so, I still like to stretch my legs and get my hands dirty on a regular basis. I know the feeling of being drenched in sweat after an intense workout. I've tended blisters and soothed sore muscles, and I know how annoying it is to scrape engine grease out from under my fingernails. I'm comfortable being dirty when being dirty is appropriate.

I don't choose to *stay* dirty, though. In fact, one of the best feelings on earth is stepping into a hot shower after a hard day's work and standing under the water as it washes away the dirt, grime, dust, and sweat. I love the sense of cleanness I feel afterward— as if I've been scoured and reborn, ready to face the world again.

Why do I bring this up? Because we've just spent the last week down in the muck and mud of hypocrisy. We've been working hard, digging through our attitudes and motivations to uncover the truth of who we are. This is important work, but it's left us feeling soiled and unclean. We need to wash it off.

Before you move into a study of the six disciplines of a sincere faith, take a moment to pray, confess, and ask God to wash away the dirtiness and distaste that come with the knowledge of your own hypocrisy. Ask Him to make you clean and ready for this journey toward authenticity.

As you move forward, remember that each of these disciplines is intended not to be an intimidating obstacle between you and God but a way of deepening intimacy with the One who has called you to be His child and wants the best for you. We'll start with the discipline of personal Bible study.

THE JOURNEY TOWARD AUTHENTICITY

First times are often memorable moments for us as human beings. You can probably identify off the top of your head some of your favorite first times in life—new experiences that came to have special significance for you and the people you shared them with.

You're probably thinking about some of those first times right now. Maybe it's the first time you held hands with your spouse. Maybe it's the first time you read a book or watched a movie that influenced you in a major way. Maybe it's the first time you tried a certain food or visited your favorite restaurant. The possibilities are almost endless.

What are some of your favorite first times in recent years?

What are some first times you're still waiting to experience?

I have a few first times of my own. Some of those moments were unforgettable right off the bat, like the times I first saw the Grand Canyon and Niagara Falls. Other moments have become remarkable in hindsight because of everything that came after, like the first time I discovered the joy of playing a musical instrument. Another was the first time I experienced the power of personal Bible study.

QUIET TIMES

When I was about 15 years old, I was introduced to a tool developed by Jack Wyrtzen's Word of Life ministry called *Quiet Time Journal*. It was a simple method of tracking personal time spent in Bible study throughout the week. Every day's entry invited you to ask the same three basic questions about the Bible texts you were reading:

1. What does it say?

2. What does it mean?

3. How does it apply to your life?

More than 35 years later, I still ask those questions when I study God's Word in private. I also ask them when I open the Bible with our church each week. Indeed, my sermons (and much of this study) are composed of repeated sequences of these questions because they serve so well as a link between the written Word and the lived Word.

Which tools have been most helpful in your own efforts to study God's Word?

Part of my history with quiet times has to do with how easily we turn the freedoms offered by a spiritual discipline into guilt-ridden hypocrisy driven by legalism. I clearly remember some of the feelings I had after using *Quiet Time Journal* for a while. In order to keep up the daily pace, I sometimes had to do three or four quiet times a day so that I could catch up for the times I'd missed.

Yet even as I tried to follow the schedule, I knew I was missing the purpose. God never said, "Seven days you shall have a quiet time, and you shall not rest from it." Relationships are regular and intimate, but they're not mechanical. A healthy pattern isn't rigid. My wife likes to have a date night each week, but she doesn't hate me if we miss one. There's much more at stake in my relationships with my wife and with God than slavishly adhering to a calendar. Regularity is an important factor, but it's not the whole picture.

The lessons from my own personal Bible study have led me to conclude that people who average five solid times in God's Word each week are probably growing in their faith. The Scriptures don't lay out a definite schedule, so the study habits we create for ourselves need to serve the primary purpose of consistent time with God in His Word. If they become a discouraging weight, they aren't serving their purpose: to facilitate our growing to love our Heavenly Father more and more.

What's your reaction to the statements in the previous paragraph?

Are you satisfied with your current pace in studying God's Word? Explain.

MOVING FORWARD

Our ultimate goal in personal Bible study is to saturate our minds with God's Word. I love the description in Psalm 1 of what that looks like:

Blessed is the man
who walks not in the counsel of the wicked,
nor stands in the way of sinners,
nor sits in the seat of scoffers;
but his delight is in the law of the LORD,
and on his law he meditates day and night.
He is like a tree
planted by streams of water
that yields its fruit in its season,
and its leaf does not wither.
In all that he does, he prospers. Psalm 1:1-3

Describe some ways you've prospered as a result of personal Bible study.

What fruit would you like to experience as a result of personal Bible study?

Remember, a journey toward authenticity isn't something we feel first; it's something we do. Spiritual disciplines are things we do to enter God's presence and allow Him to change us. We need to start by taking action, and then our feelings will come later. With that in mind, we're going to explore three specific actions we can take in relation to personal Bible study over the next three days:

1. Pick it up.

2. Size it up.

3. Eat it up.

These are the steps we'll take to develop the discipline of studying God's Word. Are you ready? Let's go!

PICK IT UP

I need you to grab your Bible. Right now. Whether you've got a huge study Bible with hundreds of illustrations or an electronic version of the text on your smartphone, don't go any further into this study until you're physically holding a copy of God's Word in your hands.

Got it? Good. Now take a minute to reflect on what you're holding. You've got in your hands the best-selling, most impactful, most controversial, most loved, and most needed Book of all time. It's more than a Book, though. It's a collection of books written by more than 40 different human authors over an approximate period of two thousand years—all inspired and orchestrated by the Holy Spirit.

In other words, what you're holding in your hand is a miracle of staggering proportions. Do you understand that?

What words best summarize your attitude toward the Bible?

The first step in developing the discipline of personal Bible study is to actually pick up the Bible and study it. There's no other way. We need firsthand experience of the miracle that is God's Word.

Are you getting that experience? Are you regularly picking up the Bible and studying it?

What does your usual habit of Bible study look like?

I know it can be challenging to maintain the discipline of studying God's Word. I know life gets in the way and you have a million other things fighting for your time and attention. But if you want to be an authentic Christian—if you want to avoid just going through the motions—you must commit to regularly, studiously diving into Scripture.

Here's the good news: making a commitment to study God's Word will benefit you in many ways. It will produce blessings in your life, many of which are highlighted in the following text.

The law of the LORD is perfect,
reviving the soul;
the testimony of the LORD is sure,
making wise the simple;
the precepts of the LORD are right,
rejoicing the heart;
the commandment of the LORD is pure,
enlightening the eyes;
the fear of the LORD is clean,
enduring forever;
the rules of the LORD are true,
and righteous altogether. Psalm 19:7-9

Which benefit in these verses do you find most interesting or exciting? Why?

These verses contain six specific results of regularly interacting with God's Word. Let's explore them one by one.

THE BIBLE TRANSFORMS US

Psalm 19:7 declares:

The law of the LORD is perfect,
reviving the soul.

God's Word transforms us. It changes me. It renovates you. That's what this verse is saying.

Whenever I prepare a message for our church, I always keep a certain type of guy in mind. I call him Joe Screwdriver. Joe's a regular guy, just kicking around and trying to make life work. He usually shows up at church against his will and leans back in his seat with his arms crossed. He's resistant to the Word of God.

I love it when the Joe Screwdrivers of our community find their way to our church, because I've seen over and over again how God changes them from the inside out. And He does it through His Word. The New King James Version translates Psalm 19:7 this way: "The law of the LORD is perfect, converting the soul" (NKJV).

God's Word is so powerful that it can take an unsaved, unregenerated, uninterested, hard-hearted Joe Screwdriver and absolutely turn that guy's life around! Spin him on his head. Raise him up a new person. Arms that were folded get lifted up, and lips once sealed now sing out praise to God.

What are the primary ways you've been transformed through God's Word?

In what ways have you been affected by God's Word in recent months?

THE BIBLE GIVES US WISDOM

Psalm 19:7 also says:

*The testimony of the LORD is sure,
making wise the simple.*

I like that word *sure*. It can also be translated *trustworthy*. The Bible is the real thing; it's authentic and consistent with God's character. His Word is reliable.

It's a good thing that God's Word has the power to make wise the simple, because there are a lot of simple men and women in today's world. Such people are naïve and foolish; they have unguarded minds and are easily led astray. These are the people who encounter someone charismatic and think, *I'm going to follow this guy now. He's on all of the talk shows. I was just at Barnes & Noble and picked up his best-selling how-to-fix-my-life book. I hope it will finally do it for me.*

When have you been influenced or led astray by a personality or an ideal that ultimately proved hollow?

What does it mean for a person to be wise?

When the Bible talks about wisdom, it refers to spiritual wisdom. Someone is wise who chooses to follow God, living by His standards and commands instead of the empty, destructive ways of the world. Thankfully, the testimonies of the Lord are so sure that they can take foolish, vacillating, undiscerning people—even someone like you or me— and make them wise.

THE BIBLE BRINGS US JOY

Psalm 19:8 begins this way:

The precepts of the LORD are right,
rejoicing the heart.

I love reading those words because they describe my own experiences as a young man. I was a stupid, foolish, pot-smoking, rebellious teenager. The first big change in me came when I gave the Bible a chance. And God's Word gave me joy I'd never had before. Reading the Bible allowed me to experience what the disciples experienced as they walked with Jesus on the road to Emmaus.

Read Luke 24:13-32. What strikes you as most interesting in these verses?

When have you felt your heart burn inside you in response to a new understanding of a Scripture passage?

God's Word transforms us, gives us wisdom, and brings us joy. But there's more!

THE BIBLE DISPELS THE DARKNESS

I love this statement:

The commandment of the LORD is pure,
enlightening the eyes. Psalm 19:8

The word translated *pure* in this verse could also be translated *clear*. That's closer to the intent in the original language: God's Word has clarity. It's not cloudy or uncertain.

The Bible isn't a puzzle. It's clear. You can understand it. It yields its message to attentive, diligent readers. Be done with people who've put the Bible on such a high shelf that you feel you can't get to it. God gave us His Word for our understanding and instruction. *You* can understand the Bible. *You* can grasp it. *You* can comprehend it, be blessed by it, and be changed by it.

> **How do you respond to the idea that the Bible speaks clearly to those who put forth the effort to study it?**

> **What obstacles commonly hinder you from gaining a better understanding of God's Word?**

Once we begin to understand the truths in Scripture, we experience wonderful moments of enlightenment. Those truths push out the darkness that used to cloud our vision and muddy our thoughts. God's Word is light that God has given to dispel the darkness of confusion and uncertainty. Pick it up!

THE BIBLE ADDS STABILITY

Psalm 19:9 reminds us:

The fear of the LORD is clean,
enduring forever.

A response to God that the Bible calls the fear of the Lord is just that: fear. Don't let anybody tell you it's simply respect for God. Our response to God *becomes* respect, but it begins as fear if we really grasp who He is. The fear of the Lord is the attitude of a heart that seeks to be in a right relationship with the almighty, all-knowing, holy God.

> **Do you have the fear of the Lord? Explain.**

Psalm 19:9 says the fear of the Lord is clean; that is, it's without blemish, undiminished, consistently uncompromised, without dilution or defilement. It's full strength. It's not watered down. It's pure. As a result, it endures forever.

God's Word is a source of stability when circumstances shake our world. In every place, in every generation, throughout every century, the Bible has been an ever-present help to all who turn to it because it points to the sovereign, mighty One who holds all things in His hands. God's Word can be that powerful, stabilizing component in your life by keeping your focus on the one true God.

THE BIBLE PROMISES JUSTICE

The rules of the LORD are true,
and righteous altogether. Psalm 19:9

The word *rules* in this verse means *rulings* or *declarations*. These are God's verdicts—His pronouncements and decisive actions. When people choose to do wrong, God administers consequences and ultimately judgment. When people turn from sin, repent, and believe, God dispenses grace.

God's Word promises justice. And that's something I resonate with in my own heart. I long for justice in this world. If I see something wrong, I want to make it right. When I read the paper or watch the news and hear about rape, murder, or kidnapping, I cry to God for justice: "Fix this, Lord!"

When do you most keenly desire justice?

How have you seen judgment and justice reflected in God's Word?

If your heart longs for justice, you need to understand that God's Word makes certain pronouncements; it explains what God thinks about this world and what He will do about it. The Word of God shows us that the judgments of the Lord are true. He *will* make things right. Sin *will* be stopped—permanently.

Pick it up. Get God's Word in your hands. Engage with the Scriptures and search out the treasures that wait for you there.

SIZE IT UP

We're talking about the Bible this week. Specifically, we're working to gain a better understanding of what it means to study the Bible as a spiritual discipline.

I know the question that's on your mind right now: *How?* Yesterday we focused on the necessity of picking up God's Word in order for it to be useful in our lives, and today you want to know *how* we go about studying that Word. Right?

We're certainly going to explore how to study the Bible but not yet. Before we go there, I want to dig deeper into what the Bible has to say about itself. Why? Because you've got to know what you're holding in your hands in order to appreciate the potential it holds to transform your life. So today we'll look at several passages of Scripture that describe certain effects or works that God's Word can produce in our lives.

GOD'S WORD IS A FIRE

Check out this statement from the prophet Jeremiah:

Thus says the LORD, the God of hosts:
"Because you have spoken this word,
behold, I am making my words in your mouth a fire,
and this people wood, and the fire shall consume them." Jeremiah 5:14

What do you think it would mean for Jeremiah's words to be a fire?

What words or phrases do you typically associate with fire?

This Word—this Book God gave us—is fire. It's hot. It's aggressive. It's consuming. The message is purifying. It's not to be trifled with. In Jeremiah's mouth God's words would be a consuming fire that would bring judgment on the rebellious nation of Judah.

I can't tell you how often I've come to God's Word when my mind was in a muddle—when my brain was filled with straw, cobwebs, and dust. But God's Word vaporizes the nonsense in my thinking and gets me on subject and on task. Scripture consumes all obstacles in its path, burning away the dross and blowing through whatever is useless. That's the idea of God's Word as a consuming and cleansing fire.

It makes sense to apply the image of fire to God's Word, because the same image is connected with God Himself throughout the Bible.

> **Record what the following passages teach about the nature of God.**
>
> **DEUTERONOMY 4:23-24**
>
> **DEUTERONOMY 5:24-27**
>
> **EZEKIEL 20:45-48**

GOD'S WORD IS A SWORD

I love this passage from the Book of Hebrews:

The word of God is living and active, sharper than any two-edged sword, piercing to the division of soul and of spirit, of joints and of marrow, and discerning the thoughts and intentions of the heart. Hebrews 4:12

> **In what way is God's Word like a sword?**

Many Christians—myself included—have a tendency to get knocked off track when we think deeply or engage in conversations about the truths of life. Whether in our homes, in the marketplace, or in a small group, we get pulled into tangents, secondary discussions, and trivial matters that distract us from the essential truths God wants us to realize and the important experiences He wants us to have.

This is a legitimate problem in the church today, and the best solution is God's Word. That's because the Bible is a sword. The Word of God cuts through the distractions and gets to the truth. Like a scalpel in the hands of a doctor, God's Word cuts right to the heart of the matter when we let it speak into our lives, revealing our deepest desires and motives. It separates what should be from what shouldn't be in our thoughts and spirit—something that can be quite shocking when we first experience it.

When have you been pierced by the truth of God's Word?

What often causes you to become sidetracked when studying the Bible alone? In a group?

GOD'S WORD IS NOURISHMENT

Anyone who observes Western culture today can see that food is a major source of entertainment. Sometimes it seems as if every other commercial on TV advertises a restaurant chain or a new microwavable dinner. The weird thing is that our culture's focus on food as entertainment causes us to miss the essential nature of what it means to eat and drink. At the core, eating food is all about survival. We make it a point to eat every day, not so that we can have fun but so that we can avoid dying.

The same is supposed to be true of God's Word. The Bible is nourishment for our spiritual selves in the same way food and drink provide necessary fuel for our physical bodies. Therefore, we should view God's Word as absolutely essential to our survival as healthy, growing Christians. Look at what the apostle Peter had to say on that subject:

Like newborn infants, long for the pure spiritual milk, that by it you may grow up into salvation—if indeed you have tasted that the Lord is good. 1 Peter 2:2-3

There's a time in the spiritual lives of all Christians when we're babies; we go through spiritual infancy after conversion. And those who are new babes in Christ need the Bible the way a baby needs milk. They require it desperately and constantly. They should wake up crying for the Scriptures, not just once a day but several times a day.

How did you consume God's Word as a new Christian?

How have your Bible-study habits changed in recent years?

God's Word serves as spiritual milk because it gives us the fuel we need to grow as followers of Jesus. It helps us stay healthy as we learn the basics of living in God's kingdom. At some point, however, Christians should graduate from this basic approach to studying God's Word. We should move away from experiencing the Bible as milk and begin consuming it instead as solid food—as meat:

Though by this time you ought to be teachers, you need someone to teach you again the basic principles of the oracles of God. You need milk, not solid food, for everyone who lives on milk is unskilled in the word of righteousness, since he is a child. But solid food is for the mature, for those who have their powers of discernment trained by constant practice to distinguish good from evil. Hebrews 5:12-14

What does it mean to consume God's Word as solid food instead of milk?

I grieve for people who've been Christians for years, even decades, yet still approach God's Word as if they were infants ready for a bottle: "I make sure to read a few verses from the psalms every morning, and they help me adjust my attitude for work." That's milk. That's not making a meal out of the meat in Scripture.

If you've been following Jesus for more than a year, you need to be involved in regular, serious, deep study of His Word. You need to open yourself to the whole Bible, not just the wisdom literature, not just the Gospels. You need to grasp the meanings of particular verses as well as the big picture of Scripture. You need to make a feast of every verse available to you. And you need to consume such feasts habitually—as if your spiritual life depended on it. Because it does!

Have you been properly nourished by God's Word in recent months? Explain.

You're wondering *how* again, aren't you? *How do I go about consuming God's Word in order to stay spiritually healthy?* Hang on to that thought, because that's exactly what we'll explore tomorrow.

EAT IT UP

Imagine driving to the grocery store and buying all of the ingredients for your favorite meal. Imagine measuring and mixing and cooking those ingredients until the meal is finished. Imagine dishing the meal onto your best china plates and setting them on your dining-room table—and then just leaving the food to sit. Imagine watching your favorite meal grow cold and congeal until it's no longer appetizing in any way.

That would be a tragedy, right? That would be a total waste of a good meal. And the same is true when followers of Jesus fail to dine on His Word.

It's not enough to pick up the Bible. Most American households contain a Bible—sometimes an armful of Bibles—but that hasn't stopped our country's spiritual decline in recent generations. It's not even enough to size up the Scriptures: "I respect the Bible. I revere it. I keep one in my glove compartment for emergencies."

No, you have to consume God's Word. You have to *ingest* it into yourself. You have to hide God's Word in your heart so that you won't sin against Him (see Ps. 119:11). That's why Jeremiah 15:16 is my life verse. It resonates with the way God made me and never ceases to remind me of what He's done in my life:

Your words were found, and I ate them, and your words became to me a joy and the delight of my heart, for I am called by your name, O LORD, God of hosts.

What emotions do you experience when you read this verse? Why?

When have you experienced joy and delight while studying the Bible?

So what do I mean by *eat it up?* How does God's Word function as spiritual meat for His followers? A good Bible feast includes at least five basic courses to ensure healthful, satisfying spiritual nourishment.

READ IT

The first course is straightforward: read the Bible. Read it out loud, read it silently, or listen to it being read by someone else—I actually recommend that you try all of these ways. Be attentive, alert, and thoughtful. As you read, respond the way you do as you enjoy a great meal, lovingly prepared. Thank God as you savor unexpected flavors from the Book He's prepared for you.

If you're not yet confident in your knowledge of God's Word, you should know that many books and passages in the Bible are straightforward, while many books and passages require more effort to understand. For example, the Gospel of John and 1 John are easy to read and accessible to anyone—good places for beginners to start.

On the other hand, Ecclesiastes, the Song of Solomon, and the Major Prophets of the Old Testament are at the deeper end of the pool. And the Book of Hebrews in the New Testament will become much clearer to you once you comprehend the story and flow of the Old Testament.

> **Record three of your current favorite books or passages in the Bible. What do you like about them?**
>
> 1.
>
> 2.
>
> 3.
>
> **What books or Scripture passages do you find more difficult to read?**

Remember that "all Scripture is breathed out by God and profitable for teaching, for reproof, for correction, and for training in righteousness" (2 Tim. 3:16). You can get there. Growth in biblical literacy is attainable for everyone.

QUESTION IT

You've got to question the Bible. I don't mean object to it; I mean read with an inquisitive attitude. Some of your questions will be directed to the text: Who's involved here? What's the big picture behind this passage? Where else in Scripture are these matters discussed?

Many of the questions need to be more personal. Here are a few crucial application questions that should scroll through your mind as you read each Bible text:

- *Is there an example here for me to follow or avoid?* The Bible is full of positive examples to follow and negative examples to avoid.

- *Is there a sin for me to confess?* God's Word will expose and confront you. Be open to that conviction and respond with immediate confession.

- *Is there a truth for me to understand?* Sometimes God wants to expand our thinking. Be teachable.

- *Is there a comfort for me to experience?* God's Word is often encouraging, especially when we feel anxious, fearful, or uncertain.

Would asking these questions change the way you approach studying God's Word? Explain.

How can you change your current Bible-study routine to ask and answer these kinds of questions?

DO IT

James 1:22 is one of the most in-your-face verses in all the pages of Scripture: "Be doers of the word, and not hearers only, deceiving yourselves." I like the New International Version's translation as well: "Do not merely listen to the word, and so deceive yourselves. Do what it says" (NIV).

Do what it says! In order to take the next step of personal Bible study, you need to go beyond reading and questioning God's Word. You need to make a plan of action. You need to intentionally respond to the truths of Scripture with a commitment to action.

What obstacles hinder you from acting on what you read in the Bible?

I strongly recommend that you record your action plans as soon as you come up with them. Write them in a notebook or journal, dating each entry. Make audio notes to yourself on your phone or send yourself an email. Maybe even write them directly on the pages of your Bible.

How will you record your plans of action in response to God's Word?

PRAY IT

I always try to make time for prayer when I sit down to read the Bible. When God speaks to me, my first response needs to be directed to Him: "Thank You, Lord, for speaking to me from Your Word today. Thank You, Father, for challenging me about this. I agree with Your Word when it says ... "

Such prayers don't have to be complicated. They don't have to be eloquent or use a lot of theological words. These are discussions between you and God. They're conversations. As God speaks to you through His Word, you speak to Him in prayer.

How does prayer enhance the study of God's Word?

How will you incorporate prayer into your study of God's Word?

I recommend praying about your plan of action as well. Tell God what you feel is a proper response to the truth you've encountered in His Word. Ask Him whether that's the right response. Ask Him for help in carrying out that plan and for opportunities to do so.

SHARE IT

After you talk with God about your experiences in His Word, be willing to share those experiences with other people in your life. This doesn't have to happen every day, and it's not something you should force in a mechanical way. But it's natural for you to talk about your reactions to something as powerful as God's Word.

For example, I frequently say to my wife or children, "I got this out of the Word today. I've been studying that passage, and this is what it's meant to me." Doing so helps me internalize and apply what God says to me; when I put the lesson into words for others, I reteach the lesson to myself.

When are you most likely to share something from God's Word with a friend or a family member?

What steps can you take to share the results of your Bible study more often?

Read God's Word regularly. Ask questions of God's Word to gain a deeper understanding of how it applies to your life. Make plans to apply what you learn. Pray about what you learn. And share these experiences with others. These are the foundations of healthy, disciplined personal Bible study. We'll practice these skills tomorrow.

DAY 5

GOD'S WORD AND YOU

This week I've introduced you to the discipline of personal Bible study. Anyone who wants to lead an authentic Christian life will develop a practice of seeking regular input from God's Word. I couldn't be more excited about the possibility that a number of people will take this significant step for the first time or perhaps recommit themselves to this discipline after an extended absence.

What about you? Will you be engaged in God's Word this week? Will you pick it up, size it up, and eat it up?

There's no time like the present to begin the discipline of Bible study. Below you'll find an outline for a five-course feast on God's Word, based on the steps we examined in yesterday's material. The only things missing are your thoughts, your questions, your plans, your prayers, and your willingness to share what you learn.

I hope you're hungry!

READ IT

Spend a few minutes reading and rereading the first half of John 1. Before you start, move to a place and a position that help you pay attention to the text. For example, I like to sit in a chair with the Scripture on a desk in front of me. I lean forward to read. I keep a pen in my hand and a journal close by to write down my thoughts and reactions.

I also say a brief prayer before I read, asking God to bless my experience with His Word and to nourish my soul in a way that only He can. I recommend that you do the same.

Here's the text when you're ready.

In the beginning was the Word, and the Word was with God, and the Word was God. He was in the beginning with God. All things were made through him, and without him was not any thing made that was made. In him was life, and the life was the light of men. The light shines in the darkness, and the darkness has not overcome it.

There was a man sent from God, whose name was John. He came as a witness, to bear witness about the light, that all might believe through him. He was not the light, but came to bear witness about the light.

The true light, which enlightens everyone, was coming into the world. He was in the world, and the world was made through him, yet the world did not know him. He came to his own, and his own people did not receive him. But to all who did receive him, who believed in his name, he gave the right to become children of God, who were born, not of blood nor of the will of the flesh nor of the will of man, but of God.

And the Word became flesh and dwelt among us, and we have seen his glory, glory as of the only Son from the Father, full of grace and truth. (John bore witness about him, and cried out, "This was he of whom I said, 'He who comes after me ranks before me, because he was before me.' ") For from his fullness we have all received, grace upon grace. For the law was given through Moses; grace and truth came through Jesus Christ. No one has ever seen God; the only God, who is at the Father's side, he has made him known. John 1:1-18

What are your initial thoughts about and reactions to this passage?

What do you like best about these verses?

What do you find confusing about these verses?

QUESTION IT

It's time for the second course: using questions to deepen your understanding and appreciation of the text. Start by considering a few questions focused on the Scripture passage itself.

What's the primary message of this text?

Who are the people mentioned in this passage? What do you learn about them?

Describe any imagery or word pictures you find instructive. What do they communicate?

Now move on to some application questions. Think deeply about how this Scripture passage applies to your life.

Do these verses bring to mind any unconfessed sin in your life? If so, take time now to confess those sins to God.

What important truths can you learn from this passage?

How can you find support and comfort from this passage?

If you're starting to run out of steam, let me remind you that this action step is where most people abandon the text midmeal. That's why so many Christians don't do what they know they're supposed to do, failing to obey what they've read in God's Word.

So keep going! Make a plan to help you apply what you've learned and considered in this Scripture passage.

What actions will you take as a result of consuming God's Word today? Record three.

1.

2.

3.

What are your deadlines for achieving these goals?

Don't ignore that last question. There's no sense making goals and action steps if you don't have any timelines to keep yourself accountable. Give yourself a window of time in which to act. Then periodically check back over your action plans to see which steps you've taken and which you've dropped along the way.

PRAY IT

Stop what you're doing and respond to God, based on what He's communicated to you through His Word. Get on your knees if that helps you focus. Bow your head if that helps you adopt an attitude of submission.

I've found that I take prayer most seriously when I speak out loud rather than silently thinking words in my head. If you've never prayed aloud before, give it a try. Most important, ask God to help you ingest and apply the spiritual meal He provided today through His Word.

Spend at least five minutes responding to the Scripture passage in prayer.

SHARE IT

Hebrews 10:24 encourages Christians to consider how we might "stir up one another to love and good works." You have an opportunity to do that after experiencing God's Word today. You also have an opportunity to feed others as you've been fed. Will you take advantage of that opportunity?

What truths have you experienced today that are worth sharing with others?

With whom would you like to share those truths?

Well done! I hope you've enjoyed this opportunity for spiritual nourishment from God's Word. You and I are not authentic Christians unless we're intentionally, regularly connected to the Word of God. We begin to demonstrate the effects of authenticity when we develop the discipline of studying God's Word, one of the nonnegotiable practices of a sincere faith.

THE DISCIPLINE OF PERSONAL PRAYER

WELCOME BACK TO THIS GROUP DISCUSSION OF
AUTHENTIC: DEVELOPING THE DISCIPLINES OF A SINCERE FAITH.

The previous session's application activity challenged you to ask critical questions and take notes as you read God's Word. If you're comfortable, share what you experienced while studying the Bible.

Describe what you liked best about the lessons in week 2. What questions do you have?

What can we do as a group to help sustain the momentum we've built in the discipline of personal Bible study?

What ideas or images come to mind when you hear the word *prayer*?

To prepare for the DVD segment, read aloud the following verses.

He said to them, "When you pray, say:
'Father, hallowed be your name.
Your kingdom come.
Give us each day our daily bread,
and forgive us our sins,
for we ourselves forgive everyone who is indebted to us.
And lead us not into temptation.' "
Luke 11:2-4

WATCH

COMPLETE THE VIEWER GUIDE BELOW AS YOU WATCH DVD SESSION 3.

THE DISCIPLINE OF PERSONAL PRAYER

1. **Is my prayer** _ReAL_ **?**

   Public-performance prayers are a sure sign of _insincerity_.
   The secret to prayer is prayer in _Secret_.

2. **Is my prayer** _Simple_ **?**

   Prayer isn't to _Inform_ God.
   The purpose of praying is to express _Faith_ toward God.

3. **Is my prayer** _Worshipful_ **?**

   The Lord's Prayer is a _Model_ prayer.
   When you begin your prayer, begin with _Worship_.

4. **Is my prayer** _Submissive_ **?**

   There is no answered prayer where there's not _Submission_
   to God.
   I surrender my _wants_ and my sense of _timing_.

5. **Is my prayer** _practical_ **?**

   Prayer List
   Income in every household
   Physical health
   Emotional health
   Spiritual health

6. **Is my prayer** _Repentant_ **?**

   "God, I want You to forgive me the way I forgive _others_."

7. **Is my prayer** _expectant_ **?**

DISCUSS THE DVD SEGMENT WITH YOUR GROUP, USING THE QUESTIONS BELOW.

What questions do you have after watching James's teaching?

How would you characterize your typical experiences with prayer? What happens?

When do you feel tempted to pray in a way that's hypocritical or insincere?

Respond to James's statement: "The secret to prayer is prayer in secret. ... Prayer by myself is the foundation of all prayer. And I would just suggest to you that it is the hardest discipline of the Christian life."

Who among your friends and family does a good job of praying in a simple way?

What steps can you take this week to improve your experiences with personal prayer?

What steps can we take to improve our experiences with prayer as a group?

Application. Make an effort to expose yourself this week to prayers that are real, simple, worshipful, submissive, practical, repentant, and expectant. Search the Scriptures for examples of prayer, identify prayers within hymns and worship songs, or read famous prayers that have been recorded through the centuries. As you contemplate these prayers, seek to identify attributes that make them memorable and meaningful.

This week's Scripture memory. Matthew 6:6

When you pray, go into your room and shut the door and pray to your Father who is in secret. And your Father who sees in secret will reward you.

Assignment. Read week 3 and complete the activities before the next group experience.

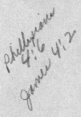

Philippians 4:6
James 4:2

TALKING WITH GOD

The biggest breakthrough I've ever had in my prayer life came from reading a book while I was a student at Tennessee Temple University, just out of high school and very far from home. In that time of loneliness, I realized that I needed to learn how to spend time with God in prayer. The book was *Discovering How to Pray* by Hope MacDonald (no direct relation). She included a number of insights about prayer that I'd never been taught before. These simple but profound suggestions came at just the right time for me.

For example, one very helpful section of the book discussed posture in prayer. Until that time I'd never knelt down to pray. I can still vividly remember places on the university campus where I felt led to kneel in prayer. When I began to practice the discipline of praying out loud, I realized it focused my thoughts and helped me avoid meandering prayer times.

But the most effective concept the author described focused on the content and assumptions of my prayers. She encouraged readers to visualize their prayers already answered as they were being verbalized. For example, if you're praying for a prodigal child, picture the event you're praying for: "Lord, I can see him returning to You. I see him standing beside me in church, singing Your praises, delighted to be in Your presence."

This isn't about attempting to twist God's arm or dictate to Him how He should answer our prayers. It's simply about having faith that God will fulfill our prayer and saying, "I believe that's going to happen, Lord." I've found that lurking behind some of our hesitation to picture our prayers as answered is the fear that God *won't* answer. To me, a willingness to vividly imagine God's answer is a much more definite statement of faith than half letting Him off the hook by saying, "I believe You could do something about this—if You wanted to."

Are we really afraid God can't deliver on what we ask? I hope not. And I hope you're ready to go deeper into the authentic discipline of personal prayer.

DAY 1

SEVEN QUESTIONS ON PRAYER

If you're a Christian, you know that you're supposed to pray. You understand that prayer is important, and you probably make an effort to pray regularly in a number of situations.

For example, you might pray every day at mealtime, "Heavenly Father, we give You thanks for this day. Thank You for this time together as a family. Please bless this food to our bodies. Amen."

You probably respond to the prayer requests of other people in your small group or Bible-study class: "Heavenly Father, I want to lift up Jason's mother today. I pray that You'll be with her in this time of illness. I ask that You give her peace in this difficult time, and I ask that You give wisdom to her doctors. Amen."

You may even pray when situations get tough or you feel afraid: "Lord God, please give me the strength I need to make it through this trial. Please guide my steps on this difficult road."

Here's my question: is that what prayer is supposed to be about? Is that what the Scriptures are referring to when they encourage us to pray? Do these prayers represent all God intended prayer to be?

How do your experiences with prayer compare to the previous examples?

What are your current goals for practicing the discipline of personal prayer?

What do you hope to learn or experience as you dig into the topic of prayer this week?

This week we'll learn how the discipline of personal prayer can contribute to a more authentic Christian life.

JESUS ON PRAYER

As we develop the core disciplines of a sincere faith, we must work on prayer. Even those of us who have grown up around praying people need instruction. And who better to talk to us about prayer than Jesus? That's what we find Him doing in Matthew 6.

Read Matthew 6:5-15. What's your initial reaction to this passage?

How do your experiences with prayer compare to Jesus' teaching?

To get a little context, remember that Matthew 5–7 contains the Sermon on the Mount. All three of these chapters are wall-to-wall red letters in many Bible translations, meaning the words come straight from the mouth of Jesus. We might think of this sermon as the central collection of guidelines for authentic living, taught by the Master Himself.

Because Jesus is the second Person of the Trinity—eternally in perfect communion with the Father—it's not surprising that He emphasized prayer in this teaching. That's why I want to focus on Matthew 6:5-15 this week. There among Jesus' core guidelines for His disciples are His how-to instructions for talking with God.

One of the first things I notice when I read these verses is that Jesus took a lot of time to acknowledge how many human attempts at prayer are *not* authentic. Much of His teaching about prayer corrected the bad habits practiced by the hypocrites of His day.

What are some of the bad habits and hypocrisies listed in Matthew 6:5-15?

Now here's the kicker: those same bad habits and hypocrisies are still present today; they still infect the way we attempt to connect with God through prayer. As modern Christians and a modern church, we need to understand and apply Jesus' core teachings on prayer.

To that end I want to focus on seven questions this week—seven things we need to ask in order to properly understand and evaluate our prayers in light of Jesus' commands.

QUESTION 1: IS MY PRAYER REAL?

When I use the word *real,* I don't mean to ask whether we're really praying. I mean, is my prayer genuine and sincere—authentic?

Look at the way Jesus began His teaching in Matthew 6:5:

When you pray, you must not be like the hypocrites. For they love to stand and pray in the synagogues and at the street corners, that they may be seen by others. Truly, I say to you, they have received their reward.

We're already familiar with the spiritual destructiveness of hypocrites. Notice here that they love praying for everyone else to see "in the synagogues." Our context, of course, is the church—in the sanctuary, in Sunday School, in small groups, and in many other gatherings. Modern-day hypocrites think, *Everyone will be so impressed with me this week at small group. I'm going to blow them away with my prayer. Revival will break out because I'm so awesome at talking to God!*

Describe hypocritical prayers you've observed in the church.

How can hypocritical prayer cause damage in the church?

Hypocrites get an emotional rush from displaying their holiness in church—but not only in church. Jesus also mentioned their praying "at the street corners." Today these people love to get to the office early so that they can be seen with their Bibles open and their heads bowed when everyone else arrives. Or they're parents who scurry downstairs so that their kids or spouse can see them praying and be impressed.

Here's the chilling part: Jesus said if that's the way we pray, we've already received our reward. That is, others will admire our display of spiritual superiority. However, God won't respond to such prayers.

How often are you tempted to seek others' approval or attention through the way you pray?

Thankfully, Jesus didn't stop there. He also gave us practical advice on how to better communicate with God:

When you pray, go into your room and shut the door and pray to your Father who is in secret. And your Father who sees in secret will reward you. Matthew 6:6

The secret to prayer is prayer in secret. And as painful as it is to say it, the litmus test for the vitality of your spiritual life is what's happening in that private place that only you and God know about. Everything else that happens in your spiritual life, if it's genuine, is rooted in what goes on just between you and God.

Are you satisfied with your private communication with God? Explain.

What obstacles prevent you from spending more time praying to God in secret?

The prayer closet ensures that we don't show off when we pray. Solitary prayer, seen only by you, is a mark of your sincerity. After all, who goes by himself into a room with the door closed and gets on his knees to *fake* it? No one does that! No one pretends in secret—so that's why God told us to pray in secret.

What God doesn't want are repetitious, over-and-over, same-thing prayers: "Thank You for this day." "Bless this food to our bodies." Most religions promote some kind of praying, and many teach their followers to choose a prayer (even the Lord's Prayer) and say it over and over. Followers of Jesus can't afford to let their prayer lives degenerate into mindless mush. Prayer isn't vain repetition. It's real communication. We actually get to talk to our Creator! We have an open phone line with the Maker of heaven and earth!

Is your regular practice of prayer real? Is it genuine? Explain.

If you feel convicted after what you've read, by no means should you stop praying; just stop the formulas. God is listening, but He wants to hear from the real you.

DAY 2

SIMPLE AND WORSHIPFUL PRAYER

If you want to see a negative example of prayer in the Bible, you don't need to look any further than the confrontation between Elijah and the prophets of Baal in 1 Kings 18. The entire event was an amazing act of faith on Elijah's part and a complete failure on the part of the false prophets, who had no clue about how to pray.

Things got rolling when Elijah—in spite of being outnumbered 450 to 1—challenged the false prophets to a prayer contest. He basically said, "We'll both pray for fire to consume an offering on this altar. The prayers that bring the fire down are getting through to the real God. The other god is an impostor. This is about your god, Baal, and my God, Yahweh. May the true God win!" Then Elijah added, "You go first."

So the prophets of Baal got to work. They "called upon the name of Baal from morning until noon, saying, 'O Baal, answer us!'" (v. 26). But nothing happened. Things got so bad that Elijah started taunting the false prophets and their false god: "Cry aloud, for he is a god. Either he is musing, or he is relieving himself, or he is on a journey, or perhaps he is asleep and must be awakened" (v. 27). So the false prophets cried louder. For hours they danced around and even cut themselves with knives as they continuously shouted to their god. But nothing happened.

After a full day of this circus, it was time to get real. Elijah prepared his sacrifice and doused it with water. Then, simply and calmly, he invited Almighty God to act.

Read 1 Kings 18:36-40. What's your initial reaction to this passage?

What words would you use to describe Elijah's prayer?

I love the contrast between Elijah and the false prophets in this account. On one side were 450 crazed prophets running around and babbling for hours. On the other side was Elijah, who made a succinct series of requests, all of which were immediately answered.

That's a powerful picture, and it points to the next question we need to ask as we evaluate our own practice of prayer.

QUESTION 2: IS MY PRAYER SIMPLE?

Let's go back to Jesus' instructions in Matthew 6:

When you pray, do not heap up empty phrases as the Gentiles do, for they think that they will be heard for their many words. Do not be like them, for your Father knows what you need before you ask him. Matthew 6:7-8

Our prayers to God should be simple. They shouldn't involve big, flowery, puffed-up phrases that try to curry God's favor by impressing Him with our theological knowledge. They shouldn't include endless clichés and rote phrases. We need to lose those kinds of prayers as individuals, and we need to lose those kinds of prayers in the church.

What motivates us to throw complicated or repetitive prayers at God?

The issue isn't that we're supposed to mention prayer requests to God only one time and then never bring them up again. That's not the case. We can talk to God as often as something is on our heart and mind. The problem comes when we operate as if our incessant repetition will somehow force God's hand—as if we can control Him with our complicated supplications. That's a bad idea.

Read Luke 18:1-8. What's the main truth Jesus communicated through this parable?

How can our prayer lives be both simple and persistent?

Let's make sure we don't miss the importance of what Jesus communicated in Matthew 6:8 about the process of prayer: "Do not be like them, for your Father knows what you need before you ask him."

Prayers don't inform God. God knows what you need before you ask. No one has ever uttered a prayer after which God said, "Oh, now I see!" We don't unburden our hearts before God to make Him understand. Rather, we unburden our hearts to God so that we can have the experience of *hearing* Him understand—of knowing that He knows and feeling that He cares.

In addition, don't adopt the false idea that God's foreknowledge makes our prayers unnecessary. Don't say, "If He knows, then I don't need to tell Him." True, God doesn't need to learn what's on your heart, *but you need to tell Him!* As you pray to your Father, you're exercising your faith in Him and trusting in His provision for your need.

Is your prayer life currently marked by simplicity? Explain.

QUESTION 3: IS MY PRAYER WORSHIPFUL?

As we move further into Jesus' teaching in Matthew 6, we come across a series of verses that are very familiar to most Christians: the Lord's Prayer.

Read Matthew 6:9-13. How do you see authenticity (realness) reflected in Jesus' prayer?

How do you see simplicity reflected in Jesus' prayer?

I need to make one point before we highlight the worshipful aspects of this prayer. Notice in verse 9 that Jesus said, "Pray then *like* this" (emphasis added). *Pray* is a command word, but *like* is a control and direction term. Pray like this. Jesus didn't mean, "Recite this prayer," "Pray a prayer with this many words," or even "Pray a prayer with these kinds of phrases."

I believe when Jesus directed us to pray like the pattern He laid out, He was providing us with categories to include in our prayers. It's as if Jesus were saying, "When you pray, keep these categories in mind." Each line of the Lord's Prayer points to a specific category of prayer, and Jesus encouraged His disciples to keep those categories in mind throughout their conversations with the Father.

What's your response to the two previous paragraphs? Why?

What categories of prayer can you identify in Matthew 6:9-13?

The first line in Jesus' prayer relates to the third question we need to ask when evaluating our prayer lives: Is my prayer worshipful?

Pray then like this:
"Our Father in heaven,
hallowed be your name." Matthew 6:9

This verse describes two ways our prayers can be worshipful.

1. Notice how Jesus' began His prayer: "Our Father." According to Jesus, we should address God in prayer as our Father. When we come to God in prayer, we should address Him as Father.

2. Then Jesus said, "Hallowed be your name." The word *hallowed* is an old-English term that means *to make holy, separate; infinitely pure and righteous.* It describes God as perfect in all He says and does. Notice that we don't make God holy; He *is* holy. Therefore, our prayers worship God when we express our recognition of His holiness—when we say, "We recognize You as absolutely holy."

Record what the following passages of Scripture teach about God's name.

EXODUS 3:13-14

ISAIAH 44:6

JEREMIAH 23:6

Are your prayers worshipful? Explain.

Worship is central in the categories of prayer that Jesus listed. Holding God's name in reverence and awe brings immeasurable worship to our real and simple prayers.

DAY 3

SUBMISSIVE AND PRACTICAL PRAYER

Have you ever wondered why people bow their heads during prayer? It's a sign of submission. It's a physical representation of respect, awe, fear, and deference to the Creator of the universe.

Did you know your physical posture can greatly affect your experiences with prayer? I've found that to be true time and time again. In fact, I get down on my knees almost every time I pray in private. Physically kneeling helps me emotionally prepare myself for an encounter with the divine. Sometimes I'm even led to prostrate myself in God's presence—literally to put my forehead on the ground and say, "You are God! You are holy! You are worthy of everything, and I am worthy of nothing."

How do you typically position yourself physically during prayer?

Our physical posture can lead us toward submission in our prayers, but that's just one consideration when we approach God. We also need to think about the content of our prayers and the attitude with which we enter prayer.

That brings us to the fourth question we must ask as we evaluate our efforts to connect with God through prayer.

QUESTION 4: IS MY PRAYER SUBMISSIVE?

Jesus addressed the issue of submission in prayer when He said:

Your kingdom come,
your will be done,
on earth as it is in heaven. Matthew 6:10

When I hear the Lord's Prayer recited in various settings, the people leading the prayer usually emphasize the words *kingdom* and *will*. So it sounds like "Your *kingdom* come, Your *will* be done." That's not the idea Jesus was going for. We should be praying, *"Your* kingdom come! *Your* will be done!" Whose kingdom—God's or mine? God's! Whose will— God's or mine? God's!

That's one of the primary things we do in prayer: we submit our will and our kingdom (our lives and influence) to God. We bring our burdens before Him, not as an equal but as someone seeking and expecting God's will to be done and His kingdom to prevail.

What ideas or images come to mind when you hear the word *submit*?

Do you find it easy or difficult to submit your will and your kingdom to God? Explain.

Sometimes prayer changes things, and sometimes prayer changes us. The more we pray, the more we begin to line up with what God wants instead of what we want. Through prayer God works to change our hearts, wills, and emotions, bringing them into conformity with His. The act of prayer places us in a position where He can work on us—but only if we're willing to submit to Him.

Jesus gave us a perfect illustration of submission during His prayer in the garden of Gethsemane:

He withdrew from them about a stone's throw, and knelt down and prayed, saying, "Father, if you are willing, remove this cup from me. Nevertheless, not my will, but yours, be done." Luke 22:41-42

When have you submitted yourself to God's will through prayer?

What obstacles typically prevent you from yielding to God's will and from seeking the advancement of His kingdom?

It's essential to learn that submission to God in prayer comes before asking God for what we want. Because let's be honest: even though Jesus promised that we would have whatever we asked for in prayer (see Matt. 7:7; 18:19; 21:22), many times we use prayer simply as a vehicle to ask for silly and selfish things. Many times we insist to God, "This is the way I'd do it."

But God doesn't rule by committee. Prayer should be all about submitting and aligning our will to God's. Then when we ask, we'll be asking for what *He* wants.

> Think of your recent experiences with prayer. In what ways were those prayers submissive?

The most important moment of submission comes at the end of every prayer when we say, "In Jesus' name." Don't ever get tired of saying those words and don't miss what they mean. Every so often I hear someone end their prayer with just "Amen." And I want to interrupt and say, "No. *In Jesus' name.* Amen!" Don't leave that part out. It's the most important component.

When you pray, you're not approaching God based on your authority or standing; you're coming through Christ and under His permission. Therefore, using His name is a statement of submission. His name represents all He is. And when you say, "In Jesus' name," you're yielding yourself, your will, and your prayers to your Father. Plus, when you use Jesus' signature at the close of your prayers, you're also hallowing His name.

> What's your reaction to the two previous paragraphs? Why?

QUESTION 5: IS MY PRAYER PRACTICAL?

The next portion of the Lord's Prayer is straightforward: "Give us this day our daily bread" (Matt. 6:11). That's more than a prayer for food. "Daily bread" represents all the basic provision we require in life.

Don't you love that Jesus encouraged us to be practical in our prayers? We don't have to be afraid to ask for the things we need. We don't have to feel unspiritual when we ask God to provide them. Requesting our daily bread was a major component of Jesus' prayer, and the same should be true of our prayers.

> Record two needs you've asked God to meet in recent months. Also record the outcomes of those prayers. Did God provide?

Jesus' concept of daily bread doesn't incorporate every desire that skims across our brains. Being practical in prayer doesn't mean we ask for riches or fame or a better-tasting breakfast. To keep us on track, let's look at four essential needs—four types of daily bread—we can always bring before our Father.

Income. We can and should pray for adequate income for every household, not so that our wants will be met but so that our *needs* will be met. It might not be God's will for you to have the exact job you're thinking about, but it *is* God's will for you to have a job. It *is* God's will for your family members' needs to be met. You can boldly pray for those needs.

Physical health. God doesn't promise health to everyone, but He's declared Himself to be the God who heals (see Ps. 103:3, for example). Yes, healing happens even today, and you can confidently pray for physical health. If God has a different plan, He can reveal it to you. And no matter what the outcome, He will be with you.

Emotional health. We all have basic emotional needs, yet so many people lack emotional wellness today. People are depressed; they're filled with anxiety, bitterness, fear, and apathy. So pray about those things: "Father, I need my daily bread of emotional sustenance. I long to be able to handle things calmly. I need to know I'm not going to lose it. Please give me the peace of knowing I'm going to be OK. In Jesus' name." You can pray for emotional health with confidence.

Spiritual health. We can pray for the salvation of others. We know God is patient, "not wishing that any should perish, but that all should reach repentance" (2 Pet. 3:9). Therefore, we can call out to God to bring wandering children back to Him. We can ask Him to save our spouse and to rescue our daughter-in-law. We can call out to God for these things with assurance. We can pray for our spiritual development.

Are your prayers practical? Explain.

These practical matters are all part of our request for daily bread. They should be in our hearts and on our lips.

REPENTANT AND EXPECTANT PRAYER

Have you ever been in debt? Most people in today's culture would say yes to that question. A large majority of Americans are currently attempting to work their way out of debt incurred through credit cards, home mortgages, school loans, and so on.

But do you realize there are other kinds of debt that don't involve money? If you do something nice for another person, often that person will feel as if a debt has been incurred. They'll feel an emotional tug urging them to do something nice for you to settle the score and makes things even.

What ideas or images come to mind when you hear the word *debt*?

When have you felt indebted to another person? What steps, if any, have you taken to repay that debt?

Here's another type of debt we need to keep in mind: spiritual debt. This isn't something we experience with other people; rather, every one of us has incurred a spiritual debt with God because of our sin. And it's in light of that debt that we need to highlight repentance as the next question to ask about our prayer lives.

QUESTION 6: IS MY PRAYER REPENTANT?

Jesus made it clear that authentic prayer should include repentance:

Give us this day our daily bread,
and forgive us our debts,
as we also have forgiven our debtors. Matthew 6:11-12

What ideas or images come to mind when you hear the word *forgiveness*?

This passage isn't referring to financial debts, of course. When we ask God to "forgive us our debts," we're not talking about mortgages or credit cards. We're talking about our spiritual debts. We're talking about sin.

The Bible makes it clear that God is the only source of redemption. Only God can pay the balance we owe Him because of our sin:

[The Father] has delivered us from the domain of darkness and transferred us to the kingdom of his beloved Son, in whom we have redemption, the forgiveness of sins. Colossians 1:13-14

What emotions do you experience when you read these verses? Why?

This is the gospel! Jesus died on the cross because His blood was the only acceptable payment that could cover our spiritual debt. Because He offered Himself as the perfect sacrifice for sin, you and I have the opportunity to experience divine forgiveness and a restored relationship with the Father.

The fact that Jesus Christ's blood is the payment that cancels our spiritual debt isn't a complicated idea. But God has attached a couple of conditions to that transaction.

1. Forgiveness is freely available to us, but the Bible regularly commands us to ask for it through repentance and confession. *Repentance* is the act of being sorry for and turning away from our sin. *Confession* is the act of admitting our sin to God (and sometimes to other people) in order to request forgiveness.

    Read the following passages of Scripture and record how repentance and confession are connected to the forgiveness of our sins.

    2 CHRONICLES 7:14

    ACTS 3:17-21

    1 JOHN 1:9

Describe your recent experiences with repentance and confession.

2. God's forgiveness of our sins (our spiritual debt) is connected to the way we forgive other people when they sin against us. Jesus hinted at that reality in verse 12 of the Lord's Prayer:

Forgive us our debts,
as we also have forgiven our debtors.
Matthew 6:12, emphasis added

Jesus made this point more directly just a few verses later:

If you forgive others their trespasses, your heavenly Father will also forgive you, but if you do not forgive others their trespasses, neither will your Father forgive your trespasses. Matthew 6:14-15

What's your initial reaction to these verses?

Basically, God will take our high-water mark in forgiving others and use it as the standard by which He forgives us. That's why repentance is such a vital component of prayer.

We must include repentance in our prayers.

Are your prayers repentant? Explain.

QUESTION 7: IS MY PRAYER EXPECTANT?

Let's explore Jesus' conclusion to the Lord's Prayer:

Do not lead us into temptation,
but deliver us from the evil one.
For Yours is the kingdom and the power and the glory forever. Amen.
Matthew 6:13, NKJV

Some Bible translations include the phrase "For Yours is the kingdom and the power and the glory forever," and some do not. The expression is certainly biblically accurate and has traditionally been included in the Lord's Prayer. I choose to include the phrase because it points to a key aspect of the Lord's Prayer as a whole: expectation.

Specifically, as we connect to God in prayer, we expect that He will hear us.

Read Matthew 21:22. What did Jesus teach about expectancy in prayer?

Do you expect God to hear you when you pray? Explain.

When we pray, it's essential that we believe in faith that God will draw near to us and will answer us as we speak to Him. We trust Him to provide for the needs we pray about. We trust that He's good—that He won't lead us into temptation.

In the same way, our prayers should address God as if we believe He's able to help us when we're in trouble. We should speak to Him as if He really can "deliver us from evil" (Matt. 6:13). Expectant prayers affirm that God will be with us and is able to help us because He rules His kingdom in power and glory, not just today but for all time.

Practicing godly anticipation is a part of a sincere prayer life. So let's be done with prayers sent toward the ceiling with no expectation of any reception or response. Let's be done with ritual prayers that are thrown out with the same level of enthusiasm that "God bless you" is thrown out after a sneeze. If we don't have enough faith to pray in such a way that we expect God to hear, answer, and act, why are we praying at all?

Are your prayers expectant? Explain.

DAY 5

PRAYER AND YOU

You've been reading all week about the discipline of personal prayer, studying Jesus' model prayer, and analyzing your own patterns of prayer. If you're like me, you're itching to move away from words on a page and do something with what you've learned. Are you ready for action?

Let's get started. Today's lesson provides a guided experience of personal prayer based on the seven questions we've worked through this week. This is a general guide, of course. If you want to go in a different direction or if you feel a nudge from the Holy Spirit to address a different topic, more power to you.

All I ask is that you set aside an exclusive period of time to pray—15 minutes at the very least—and that you pour yourself into this opportunity as if your spiritual health depended on it. Because it does.

FIND YOUR POSTURE

Begin your experience by finding the right posture for prayer. You're looking for two things as you search for that posture: comfort and attitude.

1. Don't feel that you have to contort yourself into weird positions to pray seriously. If your back aches or your head hurts, you'll have a hard time concentrating on your conversation with God. You don't want to fall asleep, but you need to find a comfortable position in which to speak to your Father for an extended period of time.

2. Find a posture that expresses the attitude you want to adopt as you come before the Father. If you want to express praise, for example, raise your hands and look up to heaven. If you're settling in for a time of repentance and confession, prostrate yourself on the ground. If you want to express your submission to God, you may want to kneel or bow in His presence.

Find a physical posture now that helps you focus your attitude and emotions.

BE REAL

After you find a posture, commit to authenticity in your prayer. Be real. Don't allow yourself to drift into hypocritical, ritualistic, boring prayer you may have experienced in the past.

When you pray, you must not be like the hypocrites. For they love to stand and pray in the synagogues and at the street corners, that they may be seen by others. Truly, I say to you, they have received their reward. But when you pray, go into your room and shut the door and pray to your Father who is in secret. And your Father who sees in secret will reward you. Matthew 6:5-6

Are you alone? Are you in secret and ready to speak with your Father? Find a place that allows you to be real with Him. If you've never prayed to God out loud before, this is a great time to give it a try. Simply speak to Him as if He were standing next to you. At the same time, resolve to keep your prayer simple. Don't let it degenerate into meaningless repetition. Don't let yourself throw out the kinds of clichés you may have heard people use in prayer. Remember that you're talking to God, and you don't need to give Him a lot of information about what's going on. He knows.

When you pray, do not heap up empty phrases as the Gentiles do, for they think that they will be heard for their many words. Do not be like them, for your Father knows what you need before you ask him. Matthew 6:7-8

WORSHIP YOUR FATHER

Remember to pray to God as your Father. As Jesus instructed in Matthew 6:9, you're praying to your Heavenly Father, and it's usually a good idea to start by recognizing His status and worshiping Him for it.

Pray then like this:
"Our Father in heaven,
hallowed be your name." Matthew 6:9

During the remainder of today's lesson, I'll provide some questions and directions to help focus your thoughts. If they prove helpful, use them. I like writing down my thoughts as I pray, especially the things I hear God whispering to my heart. If it helps you to do the same, space is provided.

Why is God worthy of your praise?

What do you appreciate about God as your Father?

How has God blessed you in recent weeks?

Speak with God about these things.

SUBMIT TO HIS WILL

Remember that authentic prayer isn't about trying to change God's mind or tell Him what to do. This experience with prayer has the potential to change you—if you'll submit to His will.

Your kingdom come,
your will be done,
on earth as it is in heaven. Matthew 6:10

Share with God the concerns that are on your heart today. Talk with Him about the areas of your life that are troubling you.

Actively release those concerns. Turn them over to your Father.

Express your willingness to live as part of God's kingdom. Express your willingness to submit to His will.

Still in an attitude of submission, speak with your Father about your needs. Don't feel ashamed to tell Him your daily needs and desires. Be practical. If it's helpful, record your answers to the questions below and discuss them with your Father.

Give us this day our daily bread. Matthew 6:11

What are your financial needs?

What are your physical needs?

What are your emotional needs?

What are your spiritual needs? What are the spiritual needs of those around you?

CONFESS AND REPENT

As you continue this conversation with your Father, be mindful of the ways you've fallen short of His holiness. Recall your sin. Then respond with repentance and confession.

Forgive us our debts,
as we also have forgiven our debtors.
And lead us not into temptation,
but deliver us from evil. Matthew 6:12-13

What sins have you committed that require repentance and confession today?

How have others sinned against you in recent weeks? How will you express forgiveness for those sins?

This is the end of my directions, but by no means should this be the end of your prayer. Continue talking with your Father for as long as you need to—for as long as you want to converse with Him in His presence. Speak to Him about anything and everything that's pressing on your heart.

Don't forget to listen. Prayer is a conversation, so be sure to set aside time for silent contemplation in order to hear His whispered answers, encouragement, chastisement, and directions.

When it's time to finish, thank your Father for His love and close your prayer in Jesus' name. Then move out to serve Him, expecting to see Him answer your prayer.

THE DISCIPLINE OF FASTING

WELCOME BACK TO THIS GROUP DISCUSSION OF
AUTHENTIC: DEVELOPING THE DISCIPLINES OF A SINCERE FAITH.

The previous session's application activity challenged you to study recorded prayers you find memorable and meaningful. Which prayers did you identify, and what stood out most about them?

Describe what you liked best about the lessons in week 3. What questions do you have?

What are some foods that always tempt you to take one more bite?

What ideas or images come to mind when you hear the word *fasting?*

To prepare for the DVD segment, read aloud the following verses.

Jesus, full of the Holy Spirit, returned from the Jordan and was led by the Spirit in the wilderness for forty days, being tempted by the devil. And he ate nothing during those days. And when they were ended, he was hungry. The devil said to him, "If you are the Son of God, command this stone to become bread." And Jesus answered him, "It is written, 'Man shall not live by bread alone.' "
Luke 4:1-4

WATCH

COMPLETE THE VIEWER GUIDE BELOW AS YOU WATCH DVD SESSION 4.

Fasting: abstaining from food for measured periods of time in order to heighten my hunger for the things of _God_

Compare your hunger for _God_ with your hunger for food.

THE DISCIPLINE OF FASTING

1. **We have little** _hunger_ **for God.**

2. **We only have so much** _hunger_.

   The attempt to satisfy self apart from doing the will of God is inevitably not just a frustrating and _empty_ thing but even a very _discouraging_ thing.

3. **Our enslavement to food** _hinders_ **our hunger for God.**

   There has to be a humble recognition that food is filling a place in my _____, is giving a strength, is giving a comfort, is giving a relief that _____ wants to give.

4. **Fasting** _Breaks_ **our enslavement to food.**

   Anything that I have to have is _enslavement_ for me.

   Fasting reveals the things that _Control_ us.

5. **Fasting can** _ignite_ **our hunger for God.**

   Kinds of Fasts

   normal fast. _Coparate_ fast. _partial_ fast. _absolute_ fast.

   When to Fast

   When you are caught in a _dangerous_ pattern

   When you have a heavy _Burden_

   When you are oppressed by the _enemy_

   When you want to _give_ to someone else

   When you need _Encouragement_

   When you need an answer to _prayer_

   When you need to _examine_ yourself

   When you need _direction_

   When you need to be spiritually _Restored_

   When you need to be _Revived_

Isiah 58:8-12

DISCUSS THE DVD SEGMENT WITH YOUR GROUP, USING THE QUESTIONS BELOW.

What questions do you have after watching James's teaching?

How would you describe the influence of food in today's culture?

What are the similarities and differences between physical hunger and spiritual hunger?

In what situations do you feel most hungry for God? When do you most desire to be in His presence?

Respond to James's statement: "Every day you get up, you have a capacity to satisfy yourself, and it's finite. It's not infinite. It's limited. You have a finite capacity to feed."

How can we identify when we're enslaved by something other than God? What are the symptoms of that condition?

What do you hope to achieve or experience in the near future through the discipline of fasting?

Application. Review the different situations described in the "When to Fast" section of the viewer guide on the previous page. Choose which situation is most pressing in your life today and then commit to address it through the discipline of fasting. Be prepared to discuss your experiences at the next group session.

Note: If you haven't recently fasted, it's recommended that you begin with a normal or partial fast for no longer than 24 hours.

This week's Scripture memory. 1 Peter 2:11

Beloved, I urge you as sojourners and exiles to abstain from the passions of the flesh, which wage war against your soul.

Assignment. Read week 4 and complete the activities before the next group experience.

HUNGER FOR GOD

At the time we planted Harvest Bible Chapel, I regularly practiced several spiritual disciplines. I devoted myself to personal Bible study in order to understand what it meant for the church to operate as God intended. I prayed many times each day. I had a deep appreciation for worship. I experienced the blessings of fellowship with my associate pastor and a core team of early members.

Yet before I dived into planting a church, I'd never practiced the discipline of fasting. Yes, I was vaguely aware that many followers of Jesus had used this exercise, but it was foreign to me. The idea was like an exotic food I kept hearing about but had never tried.

Then things got rolling with Harvest Bible Chapel. As the weight of ministry settled on my shoulders, it became increasingly clear that I needed to pursue every avenue of communion with God I could find. I needed all the help I could get!

As a result, I began to experiment with different forms of prayer, including fasting. Quickly those two practices became intertwined in my experience. God was stretching me into a deeper understanding of prayer, and He used fasting as an indispensable part of my spiritual growth.

One of the biblical provocations that spurred me to explore this discipline came from Jesus' conversation with His disciples in Matthew 17:

The disciples came to Jesus privately and said, "Why could we not cast [the demon] out?" He said to them, "Because of your little faith. For truly, I say to you, if you have faith like a grain of mustard seed, you will say to this mountain, 'Move from here to there,' and it will move, and nothing will be impossible for you. ***But this kind never comes out except by prayer and fasting."*** *Matthew 17:19-21, text note, emphasis added*

According to Jesus, there are some hills to climb or obstacles to overcome that require fasting. So let's work together to gain a better understanding of a spiritual discipline that can create hunger for God and move us toward a more authentic walk with Him.

DAY 1

WHY FAST?

Admit it: when you saw that the title of this week's study included the word *fasting*, the first thing you thought of was food. Right? That's natural. Whenever we talk about fasting in the church today, we focus on the act of giving up food for a certain period of time.

Still, I think it's a shame that we think about fasting more in terms of what we lose—namely, food—than in terms of what we gain. I believe this distinction discourages many people from experiencing the benefits of this important practice. That's why we'll explore the benefits of fasting this week.

How would you summarize your experiences with fasting in recent years?

If you're one of those Christians for whom fasting sounds a lot like dieting and not so much like spiritual blessing, I hope this week's study will be a wake-up call for you.

AN IMPORTANT TOOL

Let's be honest: living as a Christian isn't easy all the time. There's a tension between what we want to experience as a follower of Jesus and what we actually encounter day in and day out. That tension can be downright frustrating from a human perspective—even discouraging.

To identify these feelings, we at Harvest Bible Chapel surveyed one hundred people and asked them to name the average Christian's most frustrating spiritual problem. Here are the top five answers we found:

1. Prayer time

2. Not seeing answers to prayer (not seeing miracles)

3. Feeling that I don't measure up

4. Not sensing God's presence with me

5. Inconsistent quiet time

What causes you to feel frustrated or discouraged as a follower of Christ?

There's a common foundation for most of the discouragements listed—an underlying problem at the core of our dissatisfaction with the Christian life. That problem has to do with our desires. It's not that we don't *want* to have quiet times, experience God's presence, or spend time with Him in prayer. We want those things. We'd like to feel successful as followers of Jesus. The problem is that we want other things more.

That's what's happening when the things we want deepest down don't become our reality, but the quick things—the easy things, the accessible things—are what we end up choosing. Somehow we're just not able to get from *knowing* what's best to *doing* what's best. We feel stuck.

So did the apostle Paul:

I know that nothing good dwells in me, that is, in my flesh. For I have the desire to do what is right, but not the ability to carry it out. For I do not do the good I want, but the evil I do not want is what I keep on doing. Romans 7:18-19

Read Paul's full explanation of his dilemma in Romans 7:14-25. What are some right things you have trouble carrying out in everyday life?

What are some evil things you despise but continue to practice?

God has given us some tools to break these patterns, including the authentic spiritual disciplines described in this study. Reading God's Word would help us break these habits, for example. Scripture memory would help. Prayer would help, along with other disciplines we're going to explore in the weeks to come. But even these strategies require *wanting to*—a desire and willingness to act.

God has given you and me the tool of fasting to break the pattern of wanting other things more than we want to live as authentic disciples of Christ. As we'll see throughout this week, the discipline of fasting helps us fight against our misplaced desires and replace them with a desire for God.

FASTING DEFINED

Let's nail down a definition before we go any further: fasting is abstaining from food for measured periods of time in order to heighten hunger for the things of God. Read that definition again. It's important for you to understand that the purpose of fasting is more than just abstaining from food. It's to heighten your hunger for the things of God.

Even though fasting is on the margins of modern spiritual practices, I challenge you to find the index in your Bible or go online and search for the number of times the words *fast, fasted,* and *fasting* appear in God's Word. You'll be shocked at how frequently the subject of fasting comes up in both testaments of Scripture.

Record what the following passages of Scripture communicate about fasting.

DANIEL 10:2-9

JOEL 2:12-13

ACTS 14:21-23

Jesus was a fan of fasting, by the way. He taught about it (see Matt. 6:16-17, for example). More importantly, He had personal experience with the discipline of fasting:

Jesus, full of the Holy Spirit, returned from the Jordan and was led by the Spirit in the wilderness for forty days, being tempted by the devil. And he ate nothing during those days. And when they were ended, he was hungry. Luke 4:1-2

In Matthew 5:6 Jesus said, "Blessed are those who hunger and thirst for righteousness, for they shall be satisfied." He highlighted the core problem we've explored today—that we lack a true hunger for God. We're too easily satisfied by the temporary pleasures and distractions of this world.

Would you describe yourself as someone who hungers and thirsts for righteousness? Explain.

Fasting can help shift our focus from the world onto the things of God. As we seek to develop the disciplines of a sincere faith, we may find that fasting is the key to stirring a hunger for God within us.

UNDERSTANDING HUNGER

Wilbur Rees wrote a book back in 1971 called *$3 Worth of God*. In it he expressed a common sentiment:

I would like to buy $3 worth of God, please. Not enough to explode my soul or disturb my sleep, but just enough to equal a cup of warm milk or a snooze in the sunshine. I want ecstasy, not transformation. I want the warmth of the womb, not a new birth. I want a pound of the eternal in a paper sack, please. I would like to buy $3 worth of God.[1]

We'll have to adjust that figure for inflation over the past three decades or so. If we go with the typical cost of a value meal at a fast-food restaurant, we're probably talking about seven or eight dollars' worth of God. But the principle is the same: we have a serious lack of desire for God.

What kinds of experiences would qualify as "$3 worth of God"?

Why are these kinds of experiences appealing?

This is the problem we uncovered yesterday: many Christians don't desire God more than they desire the pleasures of our world. We don't hunger for God. Today I want to get a little deeper into the *why* questions: Why don't we develop more of a hunger for God as we try to live for Him? Why are we satisfied by lesser pursuits? We'll explore those questions through two concepts that many people in the church today honestly don't understand: physical hunger and spiritual nourishment.

WE DON'T UNDERSTAND PHYSICAL HUNGER

In Matthew 5:6 Jesus said, "Blessed are those who hunger and thirst for righteousness, for they shall be satisfied." The word *blessed* shows up nine times in the first 11 verses of Matthew 5. It means *happy, contented, satisfied, and fulfilled*. But here's the thing: there aren't many happy, satisfied, blessed people in our world today. And there are far too few of these people in the church of Christ. Why?

"Blessed are those who hunger and thirst for righteousness." In general, the vast majority of us who live in the West don't have any extended experience with food deprivation. Food is everywhere. It's accessible in ample and even unhealthy quantities. We have little firsthand awareness and understanding of even the concept of physical hunger.

How long do you usually stay physically hungry before you satisfy that hunger with food?

Why am I making a big deal about this? Because the ease with which we fulfill our physical hunger—we can casually grab a snack pretty much whenever we like—doesn't apply to our spiritual hunger. We're so used to eating with so little effort that we expect to be spiritually nourished by brief sermons, little prayers, and a glance or two at a Bible verse during the week.

But it doesn't work that way. Satisfying our spiritual hunger takes effort, and we don't like effort. It takes focus and dedication, and we're too busy for those things. So we concentrate on our physical hunger because it's easy to satisfy, and we allow ourselves to starve spiritually.

When have you experienced a craving for spiritual experiences?

How do you typically attempt to satisfy spiritual cravings?

Another reason we need to better understand our physical hunger is that we have only so much hunger to go around. We have a restricted set of appetites to feed (physical, emotional, spiritual, etc.) and a limited amount of time and energy for feeding them.

Think about a pie that represents your total capacity to feed. The pie is 100 percent of all your appetites—not just your physical hunger but also your spiritual and emotional needs, your need for entertainment, your need for comfort, and so on. So you get up in the morning and have breakfast, drink coffee, and watch the news. You're satisfying your physical hunger and your need for information. You listen to the radio on the way to work, which feeds your craving for entertainment. Then you pour yourself into work for eight or nine hours as you gorge your cravings for work, satisfaction, companionship, purpose, and ambition. You probably stuff yourself at lunch, and then you have another big meal at dinner, followed by some time with family and a bit of TV. The whole day is one big feast for all the different cravings and appetites that define you as a human being. Then, exhausted, just before you slip into bed, you pray to God and cry out, "Father, why don't I hunger for You?"

Do you see my point? We have only so much hunger that can be satisfied each day, and if we spend all our energy satisfying base cravings for food, entertainment, and a pat on the back at the office, we have nothing left when it comes to spiritual hunger. We starve spiritually while we feast on everything else.

What steps can you take to address your spiritual hunger each day?

WE DON'T UNDERSTAND SPIRITUAL NOURISHMENT

So one reason we don't develop a healthy hunger for God is that we don't understand the way our physical hunger and other appetites crowd out our need for spiritual satisfaction. But another big reason we allow ourselves to settle for lesser cravings is that we don't understand our need for spiritual nourishment in the first place.

Jesus' disciples gave us a great example of this deficiency in John 4.

Read John 4:27-38. What are your initial impressions of this passage?

The early verses of John 4 record an amazing conversation between Jesus and a Samaritan woman as they sat together near a well. Jesus used this woman's physical thirst to highlight her spiritual need and proclaim the gospel, offering her "living water" that would become "a spring of water welling up to eternal life" (vv. 10,14).

Meanwhile, where were Jesus' disciples during this conversation that literally changed a woman's life for eternity? In town looking for food! They were satisfying their physical hunger. And when they finally returned to Jesus, they completely ignored the woman He'd been talking with and instead spent all their energy trying to force Him to eat. Look at the conversation:

Meanwhile the disciples were urging him, saying, "Rabbi, eat." But he said to them, "I have food to eat that you do not know about." So the disciples said to one another, "Has anyone brought him something to eat?" Jesus said to them, "My food is to do the will of him who sent me and to accomplish his work."
John 4:31-34

How would you summarize the disciples' priorities during this conversation?

How had Jesus been doing the will of God and accomplishing God's work?

The disciples were totally absorbed with their physical appetites, but Jesus was more interested in spiritual nourishment—in satisfying His appetite for doing the work God had sent Him to do.

By far the most satisfying times I've experienced in my life have been moments when I sensed I'd done what the Lord wanted me to do—when I served as He wanted me to serve, shared as He wanted me to share, and gave as He wanted me to give. Those moments remind me that attempting to satisfy myself apart from obedience to the will of God will inevitably lead to frustration, emptiness, and discouragement.

We all need spiritual nourishment, and the essence of spiritual nourishment is living and acting within the boundaries of God's will.

When have you been most spiritually satisfied in recent years?

What emotions do you experience when you contemplate that period of spiritual satisfaction?

As followers of Jesus, we must set aside our earthly cravings at times in order to feast on God's kingdom and to obey His will. As we'll see tomorrow, the discipline of fasting will help us break the chains forged by earthly cravings and move toward a life of greater balance and spiritual satisfaction.

BREAKING THE CHAINS

We're talking about fasting this week, so how about we get started today with a few motivational tips from God's Word?.

Jeshurun grew fat, and kicked;
you grew fat, stout, and sleek;
then he forsook God who made him
and scoffed at the Rock of his salvation. Deuteronomy 32:15

Jeshurun means *people of the law,* so these verses are talking about the nation of Israel. We modern Christians get additional motivation in the New Testament:

Many, of whom I have often told you and now tell you even with tears, walk
as enemies of the cross of Christ. Their end is destruction, their god is
their belly, and they glory in their shame, with minds set on earthly things.
Philippians 3:18-19

> **How have you seen today's culture reflect ideas like "Their god is their belly"**
> **and "They glory in their shame"?**

> **How have those statements been reflected in your life?**

We've focused a lot on food this week because our subject is fasting. But I don't want to give the impression that I'm speaking only to people who are overweight or who struggle with eating too much. In reality, many people in today's culture gorge themselves on health consciousness, becoming so preoccupied with calories, exercise, and the physical body that they starve spiritually. Ignoring spiritual nourishment in favor of physical health is equally as destructive as ignoring spiritual nourishment in favor of consuming food.

Enslavement to food or any other earthly craving diminishes our hunger for God. So today let's explore how the discipline of fasting can break the chains of that enslavement.

FASTING BREAKS OUR ENSLAVEMENT TO FOOD

I want to camp on this idea of enslavement, and we can do so with a little help from the apostle Paul:

"All things are lawful for me," but not all things are helpful. "All things are lawful for me," but I will not be enslaved by anything. "Food is meant for the stomach and the stomach for food"—and God will destroy both one and the other. 1 Corinthians 6:12-13

Anything I *must* have is enslavement for me. If I have to have a substance—whether legal or illegal—then I'm enslaved by that substance. And that can mean lots of different things for lots of different people. For example, do you just *have* to drink a cup of coffee in the morning? For me the enslavement comes when I feel the need for a sugary treat after dinner. If I give in to the need over and over, I become enslaved by it.

What foods or other substances do you crave most often?

How are your emotions and attitude affected if you don't satisfy those cravings?

As followers of Jesus, we must not allow ourselves to fall prey to the bondage of earthly appetites and cravings. And if we're already enslaved, we must break free. That's where fasting comes in.

Look at these powerful words from the apostle Peter:

Beloved, I urge you as sojourners and exiles to abstain from the passions of the flesh, which wage war against your soul. 1 Peter 2:11

That word *sojourners* is important because it reminds us that this world isn't our true home. We're just passing through, and that's why we can't allow ourselves to get tangled up in the constant need to satisfy earthly cravings and desires. We need to focus our appetites on our future home in God's kingdom.

Maybe you're wondering, *What's wrong with indulging earthly appetites while we're on earth? Can't we save our heavenly cravings for when we get to heaven?* Peter gives us the answer: the desires of this world "wage war against your soul." Left unchecked, our base cravings will peck at and skirmish with our eternal nature and eternal destiny.

We must gain control, and Peter tells us the way to gain control is to abstain. That word is a temporary admonition. *Abstain* doesn't mean we give up something permanently; rather, to abstain from something means to set it aside for a time.

> **When have you abstained from something for an extended period of time?**

> **What was your purpose in abstaining?**

Fasting is a temporary form of abstinence. We abstain from food for a specific time in order to achieve a specific purpose—maintaining control over our earthly appetites or breaking the chains of enslavement to those appetites. Fasting ends our enslavement to an earthly form of bondage and sets us free to find satisfaction in spiritual realities.

FASTING CAN IGNITE OUR HUNGER FOR GOD

Not only does fasting help us break the chains of our enslavement to food and other cravings, but it can also help ignite and increase our hunger for God. The key word in that sentence is *can*. Fasting can help us ignite our hunger for God but only if we approach that discipline in the right way.

It's easy for us to think, *I'm going to skip dinner every day this week, and then I'll be a better Christian. Then God will be more pleased with me, and He will give me the things I want.* It's also easy for us to use fasting as a legalistic stick and whack people with our superior discipline: "No coffee for me today; I'm fasting."

> **Read Isaiah 58:1-5. What characteristics of fasting can be practiced in a negative way?**

> **Why is it easy to twist the discipline of fasting into something negative?**

Yes, fasting can be abused and has been abused in the past. But that's no reason to ignore this vital spiritual discipline and miss the many benefits of fasting, including a renewed passion and hunger for God.

The biblical account of Esther illustrates the value of fasting as a spiritual rocket booster. You're probably familiar with the basic plot. Esther was a Jewish woman who was chosen to be the queen of Persia because of her great beauty. But when the Persian officials threatened to exterminate all of the Jewish people in the land, Esther was forced to choose between her comfortable status as the queen and the safety of her people.

At first it seemed as if Esther would make the wrong choice. She attempted to ignore the severity of the situation because she was afraid to approach the king and expose herself to major consequences, including death. But she became convicted after a conversation with her uncle, Mordecai, and agreed to intercede with the king.

Do you remember what happened next?

Esther told them to reply to Mordecai, "Go, gather all the Jews to be found in Susa, and hold a fast on my behalf, and do not eat or drink for three days, night or day. I and my young women will also fast as you do. Then I will go to the king, though it is against the law, and if I perish, I perish." Esther 4:15-16

What were Esther's motivations for fasting?

What steps do you typically take when faced with a difficult decision?

Aware of the monumental decision in front of her, Esther knew she needed to seek a close connection with God. And so she chose to fast. Not only that, but she also led all of the Jews in a prolonged fast that preserved and reignited the spiritual destiny of an entire nation.

The same can happen for you when you humbly, obediently practice the discipline of fasting as a way to seek the will of God.

HOW TO FAST

I still have vivid memories of a weeklong fast I participated in during the early days of planting Harvest Bible Chapel. We were meeting in a high-school facility at the time, and our church office was a rented space only a little larger than a refrigerator box. I had no idea what God had in store for our church in the years to come, but I longed to be faithful with the challenges immediately in front me. I was beginning to recognize how badly I needed God's help.

Desperation had driven me to a seven-day, water-only fast. On day 5 or 6 I collapsed while walking up the winding stairway in the rickety building that housed our offices. Part of the collapse was caused by physical weakness, but another major part was the spiritual realization of how little I had to offer in meeting the task before me.

Right then and there I found myself crying out to God for this church that was a dream and a call. I begged Him to work in me and through me to accomplish what He wanted. I couldn't say what I was offering Him, but I was all His. In the midst of my weakness and prayer, I distinctly recall the sense that came over me of the Spirit communing with my spirit to say, "It's enough, James."

> **When have you hit rock bottom in your attempts to accomplish your own goals through your own strength?**

> **What lessons did God teach you during a time when you felt weak and powerless?**

That day God gave me a significant resolution to what I'd discovered was my main struggle in fasting. During previous fasts my mind had inevitably become distracted by the ticking of the clock as I got closer to the end. I'd think, *Just a few more hours until I can eat.* Or, *Only a day to go.*

When I fast today, I don't set an arbitrary time limit. Instead, I expect God to tell me when I've gone long enough. Either the situation over which I'm fasting becomes resolved, or the Spirit releases me.

I've found great benefit in making the spiritual discipline of fasting a regular part of my walk with God, and I believe you can as well. So today I want to share several practical tips on how to fast as we explore four different kinds of fasts we can participate in as followers of Christ.

NORMAL FASTS

A normal fast involves abstaining from all food in order to accomplish a spiritual purpose. I also recommend abstaining from beverages that can become habitual, such as coffee, juice, carbonated drinks, and so on. Normal fasts typically don't include abstaining from water. If you strongly react to changes in blood sugar, you might consider drinking beef or vegetable broth to maintain a sufficient number of calories.

It can be helpful in your early experiences with fasting to set a defined period of time in which you will abstain—a meal, a day, a week, and so on. But as I've already mentioned, committing to a time period can become distracting when you start to focus on how much longer the fast will last instead of the purpose for which you're fasting. Time limits can cause fasting to drift into legalism or an endurance test of the flesh.

My advice is that you experiment with different time periods as you get started, then begin committing your fasts to the guidance of the Holy Spirit. I love the freedom of allowing Him to tell me when enough is enough.

What's the longest period of time you've fasted?

What was the purpose behind that fast? What did you experience?

One of the best pieces of advice I can give you is to start slowly with your fasts. John Wesley and other servants of God over the centuries fasted every week, and these experiences prepared them for longer fasts. Take time to learn the basics before jumping into the deep end of the pool.

PARTIAL FASTS

A partial fast involves abstaining from selected items of food or drink that represent areas of struggle or danger. For example, Daniel said, "I ate no delicacies, no meat or wine entered my mouth" (Dan. 10:3) as part of a fast. He targeted specific items to remove from his daily experience.

Partial fasts today often target particular foods such as desserts, meats, snacks, and so on. Partial fasts can also include coffee, soda, energy drinks, and other beverages. You can even commit to a partial fast from leisure activities like news, television, and social media.

When have you abstained from specific foods or leisure activities?

What did you learn about yourself in the process? About God?

The point of a partial fast is *not* to become healthier or more focused at your job. Partial fasts are not spiritual accountability for diets or fads. Rather, the purpose of a partial fast is to identify and break away from appetites that enslave us or prevent us from receiving the spiritual nourishment we need.

ABSOLUTE FASTS

Committing to an absolute fast means to abstain from all food and water for a relatively short period of time—literally to avoid putting anything in your mouth. There are several examples of absolute fasts in the Bible, including the fast Esther called for in a time of great desperation for the Jewish community:

Go, gather all the Jews to be found in Susa, and hold a fast on my behalf, and do not eat or drink for three days, night or day. I and my young women will also fast as you do. Then I will go to the king, though it is against the law, and if I perish, I perish. Esther 4:16

What's your reaction to the concept of an absolute fast?

Read the following passages of Scripture and record the situations in which absolute fasts were initiated.

> EZRA 10:1-8

> ACTS 9:1-9

Absolute fasts are serious business, and they should be initiated for only a brief period of time and under your doctor's advisement.

CORPORATE FASTS

In corporate fasts a group of believers agree to use one of the fasting options already mentioned to pursue mutual goals for their spiritual lives. For example, we've seen that Esther called a corporate fast involving all of the Jewish people in the land of Persia. A similar thing occurred in 2 Chronicles when the Israelites faced a powerful enemy:

Jehoshaphat was afraid and set his face to seek the Lord, and proclaimed a fast throughout all Judah. And Judah assembled to seek help from the Lord; from all the cities of Judah they came to seek the Lord. 2 Chronicles 20:3-4

What about today? Imagine that your church or small group faced a crisis or needed God's direction. What would happen if everyone committed to join together and practice the discipline of fasting? Do you think it would make a difference?

> **What issues is your group or congregation currently facing that would benefit from a corporate fast?**

As believers in Jesus, we have a spiritual heritage of men and women who came together during many difficult seasons to pray and fast before the Lord. You've heard the phrase "When the going gets tough, the tough get going," right? Throughout history, when the going got tough for God's people, the tough among God's people didn't just get going; they got fasting.

We must do the same today. The legacy of faith we pass on can't be authentic if we don't take seriously our lack of hunger for God and practice more intentionally the spiritual disciplines God has provided to keep our appetites healthy and righteous.

DAY 5

FASTING AND YOU

So far this week we've explored the *why* questions when it comes to fasting: Why should we do it? Why does it help? Yesterday we focused on the *how* question by examining four different kinds of fasts and how we can make the most of each experience.

What did you find most surprising during your study of fasting this week?

As we finish studying this important spiritual discipline, I want to briefly answer one more important question about fasting before we move into some instructions to help you experience it for yourself. Specifically, *when* should we fast?

Isaiah 58 helps us answer this question practically and efficiently. It begins with the people of Israel complaining that God hadn't responded to their attempts at fasting:

Why have we fasted, and you see it not?
Why have we humbled ourselves, and you take no knowledge of it? Isaiah 58:3

God responded by pointing out the double-mindedness of His people; they were fasting religiously while living lives of blatant moral disobedience. They were going through the motions of fasting, but their hearts were far from God. Please keep that in mind: fasting is never a good cover for sin!

But then, beginning in verse 6, God expressed His longing for a righteous kind of fasting. He spoke about how fasting *should* be done. So straight from the text of Isaiah 58, here are 10 answers to the question, When should we fast?

1. When we're caught in a sinful pattern:

Is not this the fast that I choose:
to loose the bonds of wickedness? (v. 6).

2. When we have a heavy burden:

... to undo the straps of the yoke ...
and to break every yoke? (v. 6).

3. When we're oppressed by the Enemy:

... to let the oppressed go free (v. 6).

4. When we want to give to someone else:

Is it not to share your bread with the hungry
and bring the homeless poor into your house;
when you see the naked, to cover him,
and not to hide yourself from your own flesh? (v. 7).

5. When we need to be encouraged:

Then shall your light break forth like the dawn,
and your healing shall spring up speedily;
your righteousness shall go before you;
the glory of the LORD shall be your rear guard (v. 8).

6. When we need an answer to prayer:

Then you shall call, and the LORD will answer;
you shall cry, and he will say, "Here I am" (v. 9).

7. When we need to examine ourselves:

If you take away the yoke from your midst,
the pointing of the finger, and speaking wickedness,
if you pour yourself out for the hungry
and satisfy the desire of the afflicted,
then shall your light rise in the darkness
and your gloom be as the noonday (vv. 9-10).

8. When we need direction:

The LORD will guide you continually (v. 11).

9. When we need to be spiritually restored:

... and satisfy your desire in scorched places
and make your bones strong;
and you shall be like a watered garden,
like a spring of water,
whose waters do not fail (v. 11).

10. When we need to be revived:

Your ancient ruins shall be rebuilt;
you shall raise up the foundations of many generations;
you shall be called the repairer of the breach,
the restorer of streets to dwell in (v. 12).

If you find yourself in any of those situations, you should give serious consideration to the discipline of fasting.

Which of the previous situations are you currently experiencing?

Will you commit to fasting as a way of bringing those situations before God?

The following instructions can guide you before, during, and after a fast. I pray that you'll take advantage of this opportunity to practice a powerful spiritual discipline.

BEFORE YOUR FAST

You need to get three important details ironed out before you begin fasting.

1. Identify the purpose of your fast. What goals or experiences have prompted you to abstain from food and/or drink?

Look again at the previous list of occasions to fast, based on Isaiah 58. Which of these reasons is prompting you to fast?

What are the goals you hope to achieve by fasting?

2. Set practical guidelines for your fast.

   What type of fast will you undertake—normal, partial, absolute, or corporate?

   What foods, beverages, or experiences will you abstain from during this fast?

3. Determine the time parameters for your fast.

   Will you fast for a specific period of time? If so, how long?

   If you plan to allow the Holy Spirit to guide the length of your fast, what do you expect to hear from Him when the fast is over? What issues do you expect Him to resolve in order to bring the fast to an end?

DURING YOUR FAST

I've found that one of the biggest challenges in the middle of a fast is maintaining focus. You're doing this for a reason, so it's important that you don't go through the experience by pretending nothing's different, by gorging on other appetites (like entertainment or work) instead of food, or by giving up.

Instead, allow your appetite to sharpen your focus. Let those hunger pangs drive you to God as you pray about the purpose that prompted you to fast in the first place. Diligently seek guidance in His Word about that purpose. Be disciplined about focusing on God and His work in you through this experience. Be faithful to obey any directions He gives you during the process of fasting.

Here are a few questions to help you stay focused during your fast.

What are you hearing from God during your fast so far?

What are you doing to stay focused on the original purpose of your fast?

What obstacles or distractions have diverted you from that purpose? How can those obstacles be overcome?

AFTER YOUR FAST

When you've finished fasting, don't simply move on to another day and another meal as if nothing happened. Rather, reflect on your experiences during the fast. Even as you enjoy food again, contemplate the reasons for your abstinence and what was accomplished by it.

Did you achieve your original goals that prompted you to fast? Explain.

What did you learn about God during your fast?

What did you learn about yourself during your fast?

What did you learn about fasting in general that will better prepare you for practicing the discipline in the future?

Let's conclude this week by looking at these powerful words from Psalm 84:

A day in your courts is better
than a thousand elsewhere.
I would rather be a doorkeeper in the house of my God
than dwell in the tents of wickedness.
For the LORD God is a sun and shield;
the LORD bestows favor and honor.
No good thing does he withhold
from those who walk uprightly. Psalm 84:10-11

That's a picture of what it looks like to hunger for God—to thirst for time with Him and to experience His righteousness. Do you want that? Are you willing to work for that? Those who want to walk uprightly with God will find that the discipline of fasting will help them pursue that authentic relationship.

1. Wilbur Rees, *$3 Worth of God* (Elgin, IL: Judson Press, 1971), 5.

THE DISCIPLINE OF FELLOWSHIP

WELCOME BACK TO THIS GROUP DISCUSSION OF
AUTHENTIC: DEVELOPING THE DISCIPLINES OF A SINCERE FAITH.

The previous session's application activity involved practicing the discipline of fasting in connection with a specific situation in your life. As a group, use the following questions to debrief your experience.

- If you're comfortable, describe the situation or need you focused on during the fast.

- What did you experience during and after the fast?

- What practical lessons did you learn that will help during your next experience with fasting?

Describe what you liked best about the lessons in week 4. What questions do you have?

What ideas or images come to mind when you hear the word *fellowship*?

To prepare for the DVD segment, read aloud the following verses.

They devoted themselves to the apostles' teaching and the fellowship, to the breaking of bread and the prayers. And awe came upon every soul, and many wonders and signs were being done through the apostles. And all who believed were together and had all things in common. And they were selling their possessions and belongings and distributing the proceeds to all, as any had need. And day by day, attending the temple together and breaking bread in their homes, they received their food with glad and generous hearts, praising God and having favor with all the people. And the Lord added to their number day by day those who were being saved.
Acts 2:42-47

WATCH

COMPLETE THE VIEWER GUIDE BELOW AS YOU WATCH DVD SESSION 5.

TOP 10 THINGS THE BIBLE SAYS ABOUT FELLOWSHIP

10. Fellowship means our _Common Life together_.

    Koinonia: a relationship between individuals that involves active participation in a common interest and thereby in _each other_.

9. Fellowship was a _high priority_ in the early church.

8. Fellowship is for _Belivers only_.

    Our closest relationships, our life-giving relationships, should be with people who know and love _Jesus Christ_ like we do.

7. Fellowship centers on our _Common Relationship to Christ_.

_3 level of
Surface
Personal
Spiritual_

Moving a Relationship to a Spiritual Level

Don't _Rush_. Go _First_. Be _Specific_.

6. Fellowship involves _sharing what I have_.

5. Fellowship is about _partnership in ministry_.

4. Fellowship requires _Commitment_.

Things That Break Down Commitment

1. _Entitlement_ 2. _Superiority_ 3. _Agenda_ 4. _Aloofness_ 5. _Injury_

3. Fellowship _hurts sometimes_.

    I experience the fellowship of Jesus' suffering when I take a pain that I do not _deserve_.

2. Fellowship requires _honesty_.

1. Fellowship produces _Unity_.

DISCUSS THE DVD SEGMENT WITH YOUR GROUP, USING THE QUESTIONS BELOW.

What did you like best about James's teaching?

What does our culture teach about the practice of fellowship and friendship?

Respond to James's statement: "A lot of people don't realize that fellowship is a discipline—not just something helpful but something commanded. It's not just something useful but something needed. And one of the surest barometers of the quality of your Christian life is the quality of the Christian relationships in your life."

In what seasons of life have you been most content with the quality and quantity of your relationships with other Christians?

What are the risks involved in seeking deeper relationships outside your family?

What are the potential rewards of cultivating spiritual friendships that go below the surface?

Describe the barriers that have prevented you from cultivating deeper friendships in the past. How can these barriers be overcome?

Application. Fellowship is the only spiritual discipline that can't be practiced alone, so it has a great deal of application for your group. Think about the following questions as you work through the study material this week. Be prepared to discuss your thoughts during the next group session.

- What do you hope to gain from this group in the area of fellowship?

- What will you contribute to strengthen the fellowship of this group?

This week's Scripture memory. Romans 12:10-11

Love one another with brotherly affection. Outdo one another in showing honor.
Do not be slothful in zeal, be fervent in spirit, serve the Lord.

Assignment. Read week 5 and complete the activities before the next group experience.

IT'S NOT ABOUT COFFEE

The discipline of fellowship represents the grand, ongoing experiment of my life. I'm a fairly relational person, but looking back, I have to say the Christian relationships I observed throughout my teen and young-adult years were spectacularly unsatisfying.

As a young man, I was often surrounded by people in church who were committed to getting along with other people in church—men and women who valued politeness and toleration. But *authentic* would be the last word I'd use to describe those relationships. The terms that seem to fit include *contrived, mutually beneficial*, and *self-serving*. But never *genuine*.

One of the driving forces behind my willingness to plant a church was the desire to see greater authenticity in relationships. Could we get it right if we started from the ground up? Could we see people build meaningful relationships if we emphasized fellowship as a primary goal?

In any meaningful community a shared, active commitment to a great task creates the kinds of bonds among people that ultimately produce authentic fellowship. The greater the task, the greater the possibility for deep fellowship. Therefore, because we as Christians are entrusted with the gospel message and with the responsibility of advancing the kingdom of God, we have the greatest potential for deep relationships with the people we serve alongside in obedience to Him.

I've found that to be true during my years as a pastor. Ministering with people in my church helps me bond and experience fellowship with those people. Even so, I still think we're overlooking some crucial biblical teachings about the necessity of the spiritual discipline of fellowship. We'll explore many of those teachings in the coming week.

DAY 1

FELLOWSHIP IN THE BIBLE

Have you ever noticed people can have completely different reactions to the same concept or idea? Take the word *running,* for example. When some people hear that word, they feel positive emotions connected with health and the outdoors. Other people are immediately overwhelmed by frustrating memories of pain, sweat, and tedious monotony.

I think the same thing can happen when Christians think about the practice of fellowship. It's not that some Christians love fellowship and others hate it, although that may be true in some cases. What I mean is that we all attempt to experience fellowship as followers of Christ, and yet many of us have different ideas about what fellowship actually means.

> **What ideas or images come to mind when you hear the word *fellowship?***

> **What recent activities or experiences would you characterize as fellowship with other Christians?**

Jerry Cook wrote a book on the church titled *Love, Acceptance, and Forgiveness: Being Christian in a Non-Christian World.* In it he provides a powerful description of the quality of relationships that ought to mark Christian fellowship:

In the Kingdom of God, we first love and then move into acquaintance. Love is a commitment and operates independently of what we feel or do not feel. We need to extend the love to everyone: I want you to know that I'm committed to you. You'll never knowingly suffer at my hands. I'll never say or do anything, knowingly, to hurt you. I'll always, in every circumstance seek to help you and support you. If you're down and I can lift you up, I'll do that. Anything I have that you need, I'll share with you; and if need be, I'll give it to you. No matter what I find out about you and no matter what happens in the future, either good or bad, my commitment to you will never change. And there's nothing you can do about it. You don't have to respond. I love you, and that's what it means.[1]

Describe your emotions after reading the previous quotation.

How do these ideas compare with your experience of fellowship in church?

It saddens me to say I can count on my fingers the people I personally know who are willing to engage in a multiple-decade commitment to true biblical fellowship. Today's church needs more.

IT'S NOT OPTIONAL

Probably the biggest misconception about fellowship in the church is that so many of us assume it to be optional. We act as if fellowship is something nice to enjoy only if we have the time in the midst of other more important tasks.

However, that's not how the Bible presents fellowship. In the New Testament church, fellowship wasn't just helpful but *commanded*. It wasn't just a useful social exercise but a needed practice for the spiritual health of the body of Christ. Look at Philippians 2:

If then there is any encouragement in Christ, if any consolation of love, if any fellowship with the Spirit, if any affection and mercy, fulfill my joy by thinking the same way, having the same love, sharing the same feelings, focusing on one goal. Philippians 2:1-2, HCSB

There's a connection between the fellowship we enjoy with God and the fellowship we intentionally seek with others in the church.

What's your reaction to the previous statement?

The one-another commands given throughout the New Testament also reflect the core principle of fellowship as a spiritual discipline. Romans 12:10-11 is a good example:

Love one another with brotherly affection. Outdo one another in showing honor. Do not be slothful in zeal, be fervent in spirit, serve the Lord.

How is love connected with genuine fellowship?

Read the following one-another commands and record how they contribute to your understanding of fellowship.

2 CORINTHIANS 13:11

GALATIANS 6:1-2

EPHESIANS 4:32

One of the surest barometers of the quality of your Christian life is the quality of the Christian relationships in your life—the quality of your fellowship with other believers. When that deteriorates, you're going backward spiritually. And the rest of the body of Christ is negatively affected too.

That's why we're going to spend this week exploring 10 important statements the Bible makes about fellowship, starting with a definition.

10. *FELLOWSHIP* MEANS *OUR COMMON LIFE TOGETHER*

I mentioned earlier that Christians often have different ideas about what fellowship actually means. So let's quickly address a couple of misconceptions before we look at the biblical definition of that term.

1. Fellowship isn't red punch in the church basement. Fellowship doesn't flow just because the lights are on. That's what I grew up thinking—that fellowship effortlessly happens after the service when people gather around and have cheesy conversations and utter pious platitudes. Let's blow the whistle on that practice.

2. Sometimes I hear people say, "We're having Bill and Sheila over after church. We'll watch football and have some fellowship." Well, maybe. Watching football is fun, but that's not fellowship. I'm all in favor of fun, mind you, but let's not confuse the issue. Fellowship is something a lot deeper and more substantive than fun.

How would you summarize the difference between fellowship and fun?

The Greek word usually translated *fellowship* in the New Testament is *koinonia*. This word is also translated in the New Testament as *participation, partnership, sharing,* and *communion*. All of these concepts compose the biblical definition of *fellowship*.

To say it more simply, fellowship is our common life together as believers.

When have you genuinely shared your life with others in the pursuit of serving God?

How have you been affected by those experiences?

The Book of Acts records this description of the early church after the coming of the Holy Spirit and the miracles at Pentecost:

They devoted themselves to the apostles' teaching and the fellowship, to the breaking of bread and the prayers. And awe came upon every soul, and many wonders and signs were being done through the apostles. Acts 2:42-43

The early Christians didn't risk their lives so that they could devote themselves to red punch. They didn't change the course of history because they gathered every once in a while for casual relationships. No, authentic fellowship was much more than that.

Read Acts 2:42-47. What were the first Christians doing as they "devoted themselves to ... fellowship" (v. 42)?

What are your goals for your relationships with other Christians?

Don't forget what the Bible means by the word *fellowship* as we continue our study of this important discipline. Fellowship is our common life together as followers of Jesus, and it's a vital part of our spiritual growth.

DAY 2

FELLOWSHIP IN THE EARLY CHURCH

One reason I think it's so important that we gain a better understanding of fellowship in the church is that so many Christians believe following Jesus is a solo sport. They think it's something we do primarily on our own, and every now and again we gather with other people to sing some songs or plan a service project.

That's a very real attitude among Christians today, especially in the younger generations. In fact, many believers would go so far as to say they don't need fellowship; they don't need community and interaction with other Christians. They'll get by on their own, thank you very much.

> **Do you feel a need to connect deeply with other Christians as part of your walk with Christ? Explain why or why not.**

> **When have you heard Christians minimize the importance of fellowship in the church?**

> **What reasons do people give for minimizing the importance of fellowship?**

The truth is that fellowship is vital for the health of churches and individual believers. For evidence we need only look at the early church as we continue to explore 10 biblical statements about Christian fellowship.

9. FELLOWSHIP WAS A HIGH PRIORITY IN THE EARLY CHURCH

Acts 2:42 confirms that fellowship was a big deal in the early church. Look again at the way the verse is structured: "They devoted themselves to the apostles' teaching and the fellowship, to the breaking of bread and the prayers."

We almost feel a building sense of anticipation as we read the sentence: "They devoted themselves to the apostles' teaching" and what next? If you hadn't already read the verse, what would you have guessed as the second priority for the early church? Evangelism? Bible study? Personal prayer? Worship?

No, fellowship was the second characteristic Luke mentioned when describing a group of Christians God used to literally change the world.

Where does authentic fellowship rank among the spiritual practices you value?

What obstacles hinder you from being more committed to fellowship with other Christians?

My answer is always the same whenever I come across people who don't believe they need Christian fellowship: "Wrong!" The spiritual poverty you feel, the isolation you sense, and the battles you endure in even the basic duties of the Christian life should be convincing clues that following Jesus isn't a solo sport.

We weren't saved to go it alone. If fellowship was number 2 on the early Christians' list, who are we to think we can get along without the same kind of genuine connection?

8. FELLOWSHIP IS FOR BELIEVERS ONLY

Did you know that? Fellowship, as the Bible talks about it, is only for Christians. And frankly, I don't appreciate it when people outside the church use our word. Fellowship isn't friendship. Friendship is important, but fellowship is deeper than that.

The verses that best illustrate this principle are 2 Corinthians 6:14-16, although you may be surprised to see them in this context:

Do not be unequally yoked with unbelievers. For what partnership has righteousness with lawlessness? Or what fellowship has light with darkness? What accord has Christ with Belial? Or what portion does a believer share with an unbeliever? What agreement has the temple of God with idols?

What does it mean to be "yoked with unbelievers" (v. 14)?

What connections do you see between these verses and fellowship?

The picture described here was common in the agrarian society of Paul's day. Two oxen of about the same size and strength would be yoked (harnessed) together so that they could work as one. Farmers used the yoked oxen to pull a heavy plow and cut a straight furrow in the soil. If the yoked animals weren't matched well, however—if one was an ox and the other was a beaver, for example—then chaos would ensue. The plow would be pulled all over the field in every direction.

You've probably heard this verse cited in reference to dating and marriage—and rightfully so. A husband and a wife who aren't matched in their spiritual values and goals will experience chaos, just like an ox and a beaver attempting to plow a field while harnessed together. It doesn't work.

I think the principle of being unequally yoked can also be directly applied to fellowship. In other words, your closest friendships shouldn't be with unbelievers.

What's your initial reaction to the previous statement?

Who are your closest friends right now? Record their names and indicate whether they're believers or unbelievers.

In order for us to make our relationships as deep as they can be—in order to experience authentic fellowship—we can't accommodate someone who doesn't know and love the Lord. You may enjoy the company of someone who doesn't follow Christ, but you'll never be able to share your deepest convictions with that person while they're following darkness. You're going in opposite directions.

Should we have friendships with unbelievers? Yes, absolutely. We should reach out to people, love them, and show them the love of Christ. But our primary need for connection shouldn't be met by people who don't know and love the Lord. Our closest relationships, our life-giving friendships (including marriage) should be with people who are following Jesus alongside us.

7. FELLOWSHIP CENTERS ON OUR COMMON RELATIONSHIP WITH CHRIST

Because we're Christians, our primary opportunity for fellowship is with Jesus Christ. Our relationship with Him comes first, and then our residual times of fellowship include our relationships with other people who share a common connection to Christ.

That's why 1 Corinthians 1:9 says, "God is faithful, by whom you were called into the fellowship of his Son, Jesus Christ our Lord." Jesus is first, and He's the common bond that creates fellowship among all other Christians. What that means practically is that we shouldn't treat fellowship with Christians the same way we treat secular friendships.

Do you sense a noticeable difference between your relationships with Christians and your relationships with non-Christians? Explain.

Most human relationships stay on a surface level; we talk about the weather, sports, TV shows, and so on. Sometimes our relationships make it to the personal level; we talk about our health or careers—topics that require personal knowledge and a higher level of care. All of your secular relationships fit into those two categories.

Christian fellowship must go deeper. We converse with and relate to one another on a spiritual level. We pray together. We talk about issues and ideas that are spiritually relevant. We share what we've learned from Scripture and ways we struggle to follow Christ. Christian fellowship means Jesus is the center of our relationships with other believers.

What obstacles hinder you from relating to other believers on a spiritual level?

What steps can you take to intentionally overcome these obstacles?

Believers' common relationships with Christ lay the foundation for a deeper level of interaction with others who follow Him.

DAY 3

FELLOWSHIP TODAY

My wife, Kathy, and I were having dinner with a couple we'd known for a long time. As we talked, the wife brought up a burden we'd shared with her six or eight months before. Waiting for the right moment, she gently asked, "How's that going? I've been praying for you about it since you told me."

I said, "Wow! That is so amazing that you've been thinking about that." She answered, "Well, I care." That's stunning and comforting, right? To know someone cares enough to keep you in mind and in their prayers for months at a time. That's what we're going for with this idea of authentic fellowship: relating to one another on a spiritual level and committing to deeper interactions through a shared belief in Christ.

Who are some people who care for you in a deep, personal way?

What helps you have spiritual interactions with these people and others?

We're exploring 10 important statements the Bible makes about fellowship, and things are about to get personal. Scripture makes it clear that engaging in authentic fellowship requires your resources, your partnership in ministry, and your commitment.

6. FELLOWSHIP INVOLVES SHARING WHAT WE HAVE

In 2 Corinthians 8:4 the apostle Paul used the word *koinonia* in an interesting way. Here's the verse along with its immediate context:

*Brethren, we make known to you the grace of God bestowed on the churches of Macedonia: that in a great trial of affliction the abundance of their joy and their deep poverty abounded in the riches of their liberality. For I bear witness that according to their ability, yes, and beyond their ability, they were freely willing, **imploring us with much urgency that we would receive the gift and the fellowship of the ministering to the saints.*** 2 Corinthians 8:1-4, NKJV, emphasis added*

Because of persecution and a regional famine, some of the Jewish Christians in Jerusalem were starving. They were in serious trouble. In response, several churches in Asia Minor took up offerings so that they could send relief to their fellow believers in Jerusalem, even though most of the people in Asia Minor didn't have much to give, humanly speaking. In other words, Christians in one region sacrificially gave to support Christians in another region. Paul defined that as fellowship.

I know this topic often makes modern Christians uncomfortable, but hear me on this: committing to authentic fellowship requires you to share your resources. It forces you to take an inventory of what you've been given—your money, your time, your wisdom, your compassion, your possessions—so that you can share those resources with others in the name of Christ.

What ideas or images come to mind when you hear the word *giving*?

How have you experienced a connection between giving and fellowship?

Sharing what you have in authentic fellowship goes beyond simply writing a check. Fellowship happens every time you write a note. It's your care in making a meal for someone who's hurting. It's dropping by the hospital to visit a sick friend or seeking to meet the need of someone in your small group. Actively sharing what you've been given is fellowship in motion.

What emotions do you experience when you engage in these kinds of activities?

When have you recently received an act of fellowship from another Christian? What emotions did you experience?

5. FELLOWSHIP IS ABOUT PARTNERSHIP IN MINISTRY

In Galatians 2 the apostle Paul told the story of meeting with several leaders of the early church. He'd been preaching the gospel to the Gentiles for a number of years, but this encounter was still remarkable, given Paul's past. The leaders he was meeting with had literally been on his most-wanted list years earlier (see Acts 9:1-2).

Here's what happened during the meeting:

When they saw that I had been entrusted with the gospel to the uncircumcised, just as Peter had been entrusted with the gospel to the circumcised (for he who worked through Peter for his apostolic ministry to the circumcised worked also through me for mine to the Gentiles), and when James and Cephas and John, who seemed to be pillars, perceived the grace that was given to me, they gave the right hand of fellowship to Barnabas and me, that we should go to the Gentiles and they to the circumcised. Galatians 2:7-9

This is a great picture of fellowship among Christian leaders. Paul didn't approach the church leaders in arrogance based on his success: "I've been out there winning the world while you've been sitting around here talking." No, he humbly submitted his message to the leaders of the church, who confirmed that he was teaching the right things.

In the same way, the "pillars" (v. 9) in the early church weren't threatened by Paul's success. They didn't view him as competition; they didn't brush him off with sarcasm and a superior attitude. Rather, they encouraged Paul and Barnabas by offering "the right hand of fellowship" (v. 9).

> **When have you been encouraged or supported by the leaders of your church? In what ways have you submitted to their authority?**

Also notice that this "right hand of fellowship" came with a purpose: "that we should go to the Gentiles and they to the circumcised" (v. 9). Paul and Barnabas were welcomed and encouraged in order to be sent out for ministry.

In the same way, you're part of your church for a purpose. You can't carry out that purpose until you join others in fellowship and participate with them in your mission so that others can come to know Jesus Christ. Fellowship is about partnership in ministry!

How have you recently experienced fellowship by ministering with other believers?

4. FELLOWSHIP REQUIRES COMMITMENT

As he did with most of his letters, Paul took time at the beginning of the Book of Philippians to thank God for the members of the church in Philippi:

I thank my God in all my remembrance of you, always in every prayer of mine for you all making my prayer with joy, because of your partnership in the gospel from the first day until now. Philippians 1:3-5

The word translated *partnership* in verse 5 is actually *koinonia*. Paul was thanking the Philippian Christians for their fellowship—for joining with him and sticking by him in their shared service of Jesus Christ.

Notice the phrase "from the first day until now" in verse 5. The Philippians had been in fellowship with Paul for a long time. They'd remained in connection with him through the ups and downs, the good times and bad. They were committed to partnering with him through the course of years.

Besides your family, what relationships have you maintained longest?

How have those relationships contributed to your ministry and walk with Christ?

As you think about Christian fellowship, remember that starting a relationship is easy. Continuing a relationship, however, is difficult, particularly in a world with so many distractions and so much physical movement from place to place. And yet commitment to your relationships with other believers is essential to authentic fellowship if your shared ministry is to have a lasting impact.

DAY 4

THE RESULTS OF FELLOWSHIP

Would you agree that some of the best things in life can also cause pain? Physical exercise helps us achieve health, for example, but only when we're willing to endure a certain level of pain and discomfort. Relationships are unquestionably a good thing, and yet the more intimacy we achieve with another person, the more we open ourselves to the possibility of pain.

What positive practices have you recently encountered that also caused you pain?

Why are you willing to endure pain in order to continue those practices?

We've been studying the authentic discipline of fellowship this week, and I hope you'll agree that fellowship is a positive experience. Fellowship helps us connect with other Christians through our common relationship with Jesus Christ. It gives us a community in which we can follow Him and work together for His kingdom.

But fellowship can also hurt sometimes. That's one of the truths we'll study today as we finish exploring 10 important statements the Bible makes about fellowship.

3. FELLOWSHIP SOMETIMES HURTS

Fellowship is always beneficial in our spiritual lives, but it doesn't always feel good. Sometimes it hurts. That's why Paul wrote these words:

*I count everything as loss because of the surpassing worth of knowing Christ Jesus my Lord. For his sake I have suffered the loss of all things and count them as rubbish, in order that I may gain Christ and be found in him, not having a righteousness of my own that comes from the law, but that which comes through faith in Christ, the righteousness from God that depends on faith—**that I may know him and the power of his resurrection, and may share his sufferings, becoming like him in his death.***
Philippians 3:8-10, emphasis added

What emotions do you experience when you read these verses? Why?

What have you lost in order to "gain Christ and be found in him" (vv. 8-9)?

In verse 10 (highlighted above), the word translated *share* is actually *koinonia;* it's *fellowship*. So the verse literally says, "… that I may know Jesus and the power of his resurrection and the fellowship of his sufferings."

Of course, the next question is, What is the fellowship of Jesus' suffering? What does that mean? Some people think, *When I realize how much Jesus suffered for my sins, I'm thankful.* Incorrect. Many people experience suffering—financial loss, health problems, family breakup, and so on—but none of those hardships represent fellowship with Jesus in His suffering.

Rather, the fellowship of Jesus' sufferings is a relational connection born from a mutual experience we share with Christ. The message of the gospel is that Jesus Christ paid the debt for our sin. He took on Himself the punishment for your sin and mine. He didn't deserve that punishment, of course; He accepted it freely.

Therefore, we experience the fellowship of Jesus' suffering when we accept, as He did, a pain we don't deserve. In those moments we're sensing firsthand, in a small way, what Jesus went through. We're joining Him in the fellowship of His suffering.

What's your reaction to the previous paragraph?

Planting a church two decades ago, I didn't know *anything* about the fellowship of His suffering. But in pastoring and leading a church, you frequently experience the injury of receiving something unfair or undeserved. Believe me, I've done plenty of things that led me to get what I deserved. But in addition to my own failings, I've experienced the pain of misunderstanding, betrayal, and rejection—all things Christ experienced.

I'm guessing you can relate as well.

When have you experienced pain and suffering you didn't deserve?

How do you typically respond in these situations?

When you embrace unmerited suffering and don't speak out in your own defense or don't go to war over things you can handle with His grace, you're participating in the fellowship of Jesus' sufferings. When you absorb injury for the sake of others, you know Jesus in a new and deeper way. You know Him in the fellowship of His suffering.

Christ took what He didn't deserve for the benefit of those He loved. When we do the same, we confirm the fact that fellowship includes pain.

2. FELLOWSHIP REQUIRES HONESTY

Have you heard the phrase "Honesty is the best policy"? It applies to the discipline of fellowship. Simply put, we can't be authentic in any endeavor, including fellowship, if we're not willing to be honest.

That's why I love these words from the apostle John:

If we say we have fellowship with him while we walk in darkness, we lie and do not practice the truth. But if we walk in the light, as he is in the light, we have fellowship with one another, and the blood of Jesus his Son cleanses us from all sin. If we say we have no sin, we deceive ourselves, and the truth is not in us. If we confess our sins, he is faithful and just to forgive us our sins and to cleanse us from all unrighteousness. 1 John 1:6-9

What's your initial reaction to this passage?

Why are Christians often tempted to be dishonest with one another?

Authenticity requires honesty, not putting on a mask. Fellowship means not coming to church and acting OK when we're not. God forbid that any church would ever become a place of pretense where we put on shiny faces and pretend everything's OK all the time. God forbid that we'd choose such an experience over authentic, honest fellowship that allows us to share the pain and sins that plague us.

Read the following verses and record what they teach about the necessity of honesty in fellowship.

ROMANS 12:15

GALATIANS 6:1-5

EPHESIANS 4:25-26

Walking with Jesus, who is the light, enables us to have real fellowship with one another. In the body of Christ, sin isn't denied or ignored; it's cleansed and removed.

1. FELLOWSHIP PRODUCES UNITY

Ultimately, a commitment to fellowship is a commitment to unity in the church, both in our individual churches and in the entire body of Christ here on earth. That's what I'm reminded of whenever I read these words by Paul:

I therefore, a prisoner for the Lord, urge you to walk in a manner worthy of the calling to which you have been called, with all humility and gentleness, with patience, bearing with one another in love, eager to maintain the unity of the Spirit in the bond of peace. Ephesians 4:1-3

What ideas or images come to mind when you hear the word *unity*?

Do you believe Christians can experience unity in today's church? Explain.

God's Spirit wants His church to be unified—for Christians to love and forgive and forbear with one another in all of our interactions. This "bond of peace" (v. 3) is what God's Spirit is going for in our churches, desiring that we should stay together and work together for the kingdom of God.

Achieving this kind of unity is easier said than done. But it's vital for our mission today.

How are you working toward unity in your local church?

I hope you're willing to fight for something as important as "the unity of the Spirit" (v. 3) in your church. Because—trust me—achieving that kind of unity in your community will require all the aspects of authentic fellowship we've talked about this week. And it will be worth the effort.

DAY 5

FELLOWSHIP AND YOU

I hope you've seen this week that I'm a firm believer in the value of fellowship for all Christians. I'm convinced that fellowship is the crucible of sanctification. God is constantly working to refine spiritual qualities in your life and mine, and He's determined that this process happens as we connect and work with other Christians on a deeper level.

Sadly, today's culture doesn't encourage the growth of fellowship among people—even our culture in the church. Many people today, Christians included, esteem themselves as better than others. Many people deeply desire to be seen as successful and happy, which means they're often unwilling to reveal their true selves and be known by others. And many people have a low tolerance for bearing with one another's shortcomings, which must be part of authentic fellowship in a fallen world (and in a fallen church).

That's why biblical fellowship is a discipline, not a dinner party. Fellowship is something we must intentionally seek and strive for in order to be experienced.

Here's the big question. Are you seeking and striving for Christian fellowship in your life? Are you working to build deep, authentic relationships with other Christians as you serve Christ together? Are you seeing the fruits of authentic fellowship in your day-to-day life?

A brief evaluation follows that's designed to help you answer those questions. It covers the 10 biblical statements on fellowship that we've studied all week. Simply follow the instructions, and you'll come up with a numerical score at the end. I encourage you to approach this experience honestly and with a spirit of self-discovery, because this can be your first step in growing in the discipline of biblical fellowship.

SELF-EVALUATION

Answer the following questions by giving yourself a numerical score according to the directions provided.

10. *FELLOWSHIP* MEANS *OUR COMMON LIFE TOGETHER*

How many years have you been a member of your current church?   _____

On a scale of 1 to 10 (with 1 meaning you don't understand at all),
how well do you understand the mission and purpose of your church?   _____

9. FELLOWSHIP WAS A HIGH PRIORITY IN THE EARLY CHURCH

On a scale of 1 to 10 (with 1 meaning no priority at all), how highly
does your church prioritize authentic fellowship among members?   _____

During a typical week, how many times do you personally interact
with other members of your church?   _____

8. FELLOWSHIP IS FOR BELIEVERS ONLY

Of your 10 closest friends, how many are Christians?   _____

On a scale of 1 to 10 (with 1 meaning not important at all), how important
is faith when you choose the people you spend the most time with?   _____

7. FELLOWSHIP CENTERS ON OUR COMMON RELATIONSHIP WITH CHRIST

On a scale of 1 to 10 (with 1 meaning never), how often do you
talk with your friends on a spiritual level during a typical week?   _____

During a typical week, how often do you pray with other believers?   _____

6. FELLOWSHIP INVOLVES SHARING WHAT WE HAVE

On a scale of 1 to 10 (with 1 meaning not satisfied), how satisfied
are you with your level of financial giving to the church?   _____

During a typical week, how often do you intentionally share your resources
(time, money, possessions, talents, etc.) in order to benefit others?   _____

5. FELLOWSHIP IS ABOUT PARTNERSHIP IN MINISTRY

On a scale of 1 to 10 (with 1 meaning no connection), how much
connection do you feel with the leaders of your church?   _____

On a scale of 1 to 10 (with 1 meaning no partnership), to what degree
do you partner with others to minister in your community?   _____

4. FELLOWSHIP REQUIRES COMMITMENT

Of your 10 closest friends, how many have you known for more than two years? _____

On a scale of 1 to 10 (with 1 meaning constantly), how often do you
experience significant conflict in your friendships in a given year?   _____

3. FELLOWSHIP SOMETIMES HURTS

On a scale of 1 to 10 (with 1 meaning not common at all), how common
is it for you to experience pain or inconvenience on behalf of your friends? _____

On a scale of 1 to 10 (with 1 meaning no connection), how much
connection do you feel with Jesus in the fellowship of His suffering? _____

2. FELLOWSHIP REQUIRES HONESTY

In a given month, how many times do you typically
confess your sin to a fellow Christian? _____

On a scale of 1 to 10 (with 1 meaning completely dishonest), how
honest are you with your friends and fellow members of your church? _____

1. FELLOWSHIP PRODUCES UNITY

On a scale of 1 to 10 (with 1 meaning no effort), how much
effort do you contribute to maintaining unity in your church? _____

On a scale of 1 to 10 (with 1 meaning totally unwilling), how
willing are you to forgive people in the church who wrong you? _____

RESULTS

Obviously, this is an unscientific evaluation, and the following score ranges are based
on averages more than specific research. But instruments like this can provide a starting
place for evaluating the seriousness of our commitment to the discipline of fellowship.

Tally all of your scores from the previous questions to find the range for your total score.

0 to 36   ***No Commitment***

If you find yourself in this range, you have little or no commitment to the discipline
of fellowship.

37 to 80   ***Small Commitment***

You have a small commitment to fellowship, which means you're aware that fellowship
is valuable and you have limited experience connecting with others on a deeper level.
You're scratching the surface of what biblical fellowship has to offer.

81 to 145   *Great Commitment*

If your score landed in this range, you have a great commitment to fellowship. It's a priority in your life, and you regularly experience the blessings (and sometimes pains) that come with serious, Christ-centered friendships.

146 and Above   *Outstanding Commitment*

If you scored higher than 146, you're deeply committed to biblical fellowship, and you should concentrate on teaching others how to experience the depth of relationships you've experienced.

What's your reaction to your score on this evaluation?

MOVING FORWARD

As we continue together on this journey toward authenticity, I hope you'll often return to the discipline of fellowship. It's vital to your health and growth as a follower of Christ.

For that reason I hope you'll share this evaluation and even your personal results with the people closest to you. If you're part of a small group or another official gathering in your church, the previous questions can be invaluable in strengthening relationships on a corporate level. And even if you're studying this material as an individual, I hope you'll share what you've learned this week with the people closest to you.

Fellowship is a spiritual discipline. It's a command from God's Word. And if you want to be an authentic follower of Jesus, it's a practice you need now and for the rest of your life.

1. Jerry Cook and Stanley C. Baldwin, *Love, Acceptance, and Forgiveness: Being Christian in a Non-Christian World* (Ventura, CA: Regal, 2009), 14–15.

THE DISCIPLINE OF SERVICE

WELCOME BACK TO THIS GROUP DISCUSSION OF
AUTHENTIC: DEVELOPING THE DISCIPLINES OF A SINCERE FAITH.

The previous session's application activity challenged you to contemplate two questions about fellowship in your group. Spend a few minutes discussing those questions as a group.

- What do you hope to gain from this group in the area of fellowship?

- What will you contribute to strengthen the fellowship of this group?

Describe what you liked best about the lessons in week 5. What questions do you have?

What ideas or images come to mind when you hear the word *service?*

To prepare for the DVD segment, read aloud the following verses.

> *Will any one of you who has a servant plowing or keeping sheep say to him when he has come in from the field, "Come at once and recline at table"? Will he not rather say to him, "Prepare supper for me, and dress properly, and serve me while I eat and drink, and afterward you will eat and drink"? Does he thank the servant because he did what was commanded? So you also, when you have done all that you were commanded, say, "We are unworthy servants; we have only done what was our duty."*
> *Luke 17:7-10*

WATCH

COMPLETE THE VIEWER GUIDE BELOW AS YOU WATCH DVD SESSION 6.

THE DISCIPLINE OF SERVICE

1. We must not expect God to serve _____ before we have served _____.

What Are You Expecting from God?

1. Protection for your _____   2. _____ provision

3. _____   4. _____   5. _____

2. We must not expect any immediate _____ for our service.

Don't serve for something you _____ _____.

Reasons People Quit Serving

I didn't feel _____.

I didn't get the _____ I wanted.

I didn't get the _____ I wanted.

Ministry is _____ _____.

3. We must see service as our _____ to Jesus Christ.

We are _____ to serve.

4. We must serve _____.

Faithful: _____ in the performance of duty

We Must Serve Faithfully

Even when my schedule is _____

Even when I want to _____

Even when my heart is _____

Even when I serve in _____

5. We must serve _____, _____, _____.

DISCUSS THE DVD SEGMENT WITH YOUR GROUP, USING THE QUESTIONS BELOW.

What did you like best about James's teaching?

What does it mean to serve God in today's world? To serve others?

Why is it easy for us to place expectations on God, based on the ways we serve Him?

How are you currently fulfilling your obligation to serve God?

What barriers often prevent us from faithfully serving God in our church and community?

What are the benefits of obeying God's command to serve?

How can we work together as a group to practice the discipline of service?

Application. Have a conversation this week with an individual who has faithfully served God in your community. Allow that person to tell his or her story. Then ask him or her the following questions.

- What motivates you to continue serving God?

- What benefits or blessings have you received from serving God?

- What barriers have you been forced to overcome in order to continue serving God?

This week's Scripture memory. Mark 10:45

Even the Son of Man came not to be served but to serve, and to give his life as a ransom for many.

Assignment. Read week 6 and complete the activities before the next group experience.

Video sessions available for purchase
at *www.lifeway.com/authentic*

OPENING DOORS

Very early in my walk with Christ, the student pastor in our church began to take me with him to visit other students. These visits, intended to offer encouragement, often focused on praying with people. Not a lot was required of me, but the experience of being involved in direct ministry whetted my appetite for more.

After a while I was encouraged to lead Bible studies. Then Kathy and I—before we were married—served together in a bus ministry. Piling 50 or 60 kids into a bus and bringing them to Sunday School, we unknowingly broke every transport code on the books, but we were eager to enable children in the neighborhood to find Christ. On Saturdays we often visited the homes of those kids, meeting their parents and praying with the family.

Eventually, the first funeral I ever led, at the age of 23, was for a little girl from our bus ministry. That was a sobering experience—an event that plunged me deep into the heartbreaking aspects of serving people on behalf of Christ.

As I look back on those years today, I realize with gratitude that those who watched over my early spiritual development were wise enough to keep opening new doors of responsibility and new opportunities for ministry in my life. Those experiences confirmed my spiritual growth, challenged me to serve Christ in new ways, and pushed me further on my journey toward authenticity as a follower of Jesus.

The same can be true of you. In fact, I believe the same *must* be true of your own journey toward spiritual authenticity. As we'll see this week, practicing the discipline of serving Christ has a direct, noticeable impact on the degree to which personal spiritual growth either plateaus or continues upward throughout a person's life.

Service is a believer's natural response to Jesus' love and sacrifice. It's the day-to-day proving ground that reveals how well or how poorly we've internalized what Christ has done for us. In addition, service expresses our understanding of the way He wants us to relate to others as we represent Him in the world.

DAY 1

CONFRONTING OUR EXPECTATIONS

I want to be an authentic follower of Christ. I don't know how much longer I'm going to be in this world, and I don't want to get to the finish line with a bunch of unfinished stuff God wanted to do through me.

I don't want to waste time on the minimum requirements and the "I'll figure it out later" approach to living for God. I want to be what God wants me to be *now*. I want to be real, genuine, and sincere. I don't want to look the part; I don't want to go through the motions. I want to *own* it—authentic faith.

What about you?

> **What emotions do you experience when you contemplate the idea of authentic faith?**

> **How have you been challenged to authentic faith so far during this study?**

In truth, I think a lot of people feel this longing for spiritual authenticity. I see it in their faces when I preach each weekend; they want to have a genuine relationship with the Lord. They want to feel a personal connection with God.

But here's the crucial point again: authenticity isn't just something you *feel*. Authentic faith actually involves something you *do*. That's where the discipline of serving Jesus Christ comes in.

OUR EXAMPLE IN SERVICE

As followers of Jesus, we Christians understand that we're supposed to become more and more like Jesus as we journey through life—that we should "be imitators of God, as beloved children" (Eph. 5:1). On a practical level we imitate Jesus by praying, as He did. We read the Word, as He did. We fast in order to combat the temptations and distractions of the world, as He did. We fellowship with others and join with others in community, as He did. All of these practices were important to Jesus during His public ministry on earth.

The discipline of service was important to Jesus as well. In fact, service was one of His primary motivations for living among us on earth:

Whoever would be great among you must be your servant, and whoever would be first among you must be slave of all. For even the Son of Man came not to be served but to serve, and to give his life as a ransom for many. Mark 10:43-45

What's your initial reaction to this passage?

What ideas or images come to mind when you hear words like *serve* and *servant*?

As followers of Jesus, we're called to be servants in this world. We're called to invest our time, money, energy, and other resources in loving our neighbors and working for the good of those in need. We're called to care for others as a spiritual discipline, and in doing so, we render service not only to the people we encounter but also to the Lord.

I'll tell you up front that we're not going to spend a lot of time this week on practical methods for serving God and ministering to others. I'm not going to go through the different ministries you should be involved in or give tips on how to love others the way Jesus did, because you already know how to serve. You're already engaged in service of one kind or another.

In what ways do you currently serve God and others?

So instead of addressing the methodology of service, we're going to focus this week on some principles that will help us serve in an authentic way—in a way that brings glory to God and connects people with Him. We'll start by focusing on Jesus' words in Luke 17:7-10:

Will any one of you who has a servant plowing or keeping sheep say to him when he has come in from the field, "Come at once and recline at table"? Will he not rather say to him, "Prepare supper for me, and dress properly, and serve me while I eat and drink, and afterward you will eat and drink"? Does he thank the servant because he did what was commanded? So you also, when you have done all that you were commanded, say, "We are unworthy servants; we have only done what was our duty."

How would you summarize Jesus' teaching in these verses?

These verses help us identify several principles for practicing the discipline of service in a way that's authentic and leads to spiritual growth. Here's the first principle.

WE MUST NOT EXPECT GOD TO SERVE US BEFORE WE'VE SERVED HIM

Imagine you're a servant on a ranch or a farm somewhere in the heartland of the United States. Actually, the Greek word translated *servant* in Luke 17:7-10 is *doulon,* which means *slave,* so that may be a better interpretation for the sake of this illustration.

In any case, imagine you've been working in the field all day bailing hay or keeping track of herds and individual animals. You're tired. You're dirty. Does that mean it's time for a nice meal and a break? Will the master of the ranch pull out a chair for you at the table, tuck a napkin under your chin, and start cutting your steak? Will he take off your boots and rub your feet as a reward for a hard day's work?

No. If you're a servant—a doulon, a slave—you'll be expected to continue serving. That's your job. That's your identity. The master will always be first, and you'll always be second.

That's the context of Jesus' illustration in Luke 17:7-10. And the point He was driving home is an important one: we must not expect God to serve us before we've served Him. God is the Master, and we're servants in His kingdom. He's the priority, and we're always second, even in our own eyes.

What's your reaction to the previous statements? Why?

When have you recently felt that you needed a break from serving Jesus? Why did you feel that way?

So do you expect God to serve you? Are you expecting Him to serve you even now? Have your prayers ever drifted into something like "OK, God, I just spent all week doing ministry and looking for opportunities to obey You, so now it's my turn. I need this, this, and that, and I need them now."

Maybe you haven't been that blatant in your expectations, but there are other ways we do this more subtly as Christians. For example, here are some common areas in which we presume God will follow *our* expectations—that He will serve *us*—simply because we're following Him.

- *Protection for our children.* We don't want our children to be hurt, and we desperately want them to avoid spiritual struggles. That makes sense. But if we demand that God eliminate all trials and suffering from their lives, we're in for disappointment.

- *Provision of financial wants.* American culture tells us always to upsize, never downsize. But that's not the attitude of a servant.

- *Health and healing.* Yes, God is in the business of healing, and He often responds to our prayers for health, even in miraculous ways. However, we're in danger when we try to hold God for ransom and when we give in to spiritual doubts when our prayers go unanswered.

- *Guidance.* Life is full of difficult decisions, and we often don't understand why God doesn't make the right choice clear for us. We should never be afraid to ask God for wisdom (see Jas. 1:5), but we should never demand easy solutions when we face difficult situations.

- *Salvation of a loved one.* It's tempting to try using our service for God as currency we can spend on the spiritual health of others, but things don't work that way in reality. People are responsible for their own choices and spiritual conditions before God.

In what ways have you expected God to serve you?

When have you felt disappointed with God or angry at Him because He failed to meet your expectations?

God isn't a coin-operated deity; He doesn't automatically or mechanically respond the way we want. So when our child get hurts or we lose a job or get a bad health report, our immediate response to God reveals a lot about our expectations. Watch out for any way of thinking that says, *If I do X, then God owes me Y.*

We must not expect God to serve us *before* we've served Him or even *because* we've served Him. We're not in a position nor do we have nearly enough of the big picture to negotiate with God. God is the Master, and we are doulons; we are slaves. Therefore, we must trust and serve Him—always.

DAY 2

UNDERSTANDING OUR ROLE AS A SERVANT

Have you heard about same-day shipping? If you have an important document or package, you can send it through a major postal carrier in the morning and have it arrive at your intended destination later that afternoon or evening, even if that destination is hundreds of miles away. Or if you're shopping online and see something you absolutely have to have *right away,* you can get it the same day. It'll cost you an arm and a leg, of course, but you can get it.

Same-day shipping is a natural by-product of our culture's rapidly increasing desire for instant gratification. We want everything faster. We want our food ready the moment we order it. We want payment sent electronically as soon as we finish our work.

> How have you seen the desire for instant gratification reflected in society?

> When have you recently been frustrated because something didn't happen fast enough or arrive soon enough?

As you might expect, our desire for instant gratification doesn't have much influence on the Creator of the universe—on the God for whom "one day is as a thousand years, and a thousand years as one day" (2 Pet. 3:8). This is especially important to remember when we think about the discipline of service.

WE MUST NOT EXPECT AN IMMEDIATE RETURN FOR OUR SERVICE

Yesterday we saw that following Jesus should never lead us to expect that God will serve us before we've done our duty in service to Him—that we should never treat God as if He owes us anything simply because we follow Him. Unfortunately, many Christians have twisted this truth into the belief that we'll receive no reward for our service beyond being spared the ravages of hell.

That's not the case. In fact, several Scripture passages make it clear that God will reward us for the earthly service we render Him and His kingdom. Here's a good example:

I have fought the good fight, I have finished the race, I have kept the faith. Henceforth there is laid up for me the crown of righteousness, which the Lord, the righteous judge, will award to me on that Day, and not only to me but also to all who have loved his appearing. 2 Timothy 4:7-8

What emotions do you experience when you read these verses? Why?

Paul wrote these words near the end of his life on earth. He knew he'd been a faithful servant in God's kingdom, and he looked forward to his reward. But he also knew he'd receive his reward "on that Day" (v. 8). It would come in the future, not as an immediate payment for his service each day.

Read the following passages of Scripture and record what they teach about our future reward for service in God's kingdom.

MATTHEW 25:20-23

JOHN 14:1-3

1 CORINTHIANS 3:12-15

What heavenly rewards are you most looking forward to when your time of service on earth is finished?

As Christians, we can expect to be compensated for the many ways we give our time, energy, and talents in service to God. He's promised to reward us. But we're mistaken if we expect those rewards to flow from heaven and bless us immediately in response to that service.

That brings us back to Luke 17:7-8:

Will any one of you who has a servant plowing or keeping sheep say to him when he has come in from the field, "Come at once and recline at table"? Will he not rather say to him, "Prepare supper for me, and dress properly, and serve me while I eat and drink, and afterward you will eat and drink"?

Jesus made it clear in these verses that immediate gratification isn't a reality for servants in the kingdom of God. What that means in practical terms is that we as Christians should never expect an immediate return for our service. When we give of ourselves and of our resources, we do so because we want to obey our Master, not because we expect to receive blessings as payment. That's authentic service.

Here's the third principle we need to understand about the discipline of service.

WE MUST SEE OUR SERVICE AS OUR OBLIGATION TO JESUS CHRIST

Luke 17:10 is a verse that makes many Christians uncomfortable, and I actually think that's a good thing. Check it out:

You also, when you have done all that you were commanded, say, "We are unworthy servants; we have only done what was our duty."

What ideas or images come to mind when you hear the word *duty*?

How would you summarize your current duty or obligation to Jesus Christ?

By almost any measure, some people do a lot for the Lord. Maybe that's you. Maybe you spend dozens of hours ministering each week and give thousands of dollars to God's kingdom each month. But whatever you do in service to God, don't ever let yourself develop the idea you're an elite Christian because you serve. Don't let yourself think, *People need to acknowledge me. Others need to appreciate me because I do so much for God.*

Here's the truth: you're just doing your job. You're stepping up to do your duty as a follower of Christ.

When have you recently been acknowledged or congratulated for serving God and ministering to others?

What emotions do you feel when people recognize and reward your service?

Let me get straight to the point. If you're a follower of Jesus, you're under orders to serve God and other people. You're *commanded* throughout Scripture to serve. You're under an obligation to serve because that's what your Master expects.

The Great Commandment says, "You shall love the Lord your God" and "You shall love your neighbor as yourself" (Matt. 22:37,39). The Great Commission says:

Go therefore and make disciples of all nations, baptizing them in the name of the Father and of the Son and of the Holy Spirit, teaching them to observe all that I have commanded you. Matthew 28:19-20

Serving God in these ways is not only obedience to Jesus' commands but also a response to the sacrifice He made for your salvation. Because of the difference Jesus has made in your life, you want to actively love Him, actively love other people, and continually work to make disciples for His kingdom.

That means you don't need to pray about the discipline of service. You don't need to gather a think tank and spend a lot of time talking about the discipline of service. You don't need to contemplate personally whether you should serve or whether your efforts are best spent elsewhere. Just do it. Roll up your sleeves and get to work, just like Jesus:

Even the Son of Man came not to be served but to serve, and to give his life as a ransom for many. Mark 10:45

In what situations have you most successfully served God and ministered to others in the past?

Where are some opportunities for you to serve God this week?

SERVING FAITHFULLY

Lots of awards and accolades are given to those who excel in our culture. During a high-school graduation, for example, the person who's done the best academic work becomes the valedictorian. In college we can recognize the people who've achieved the highest levels of academic success because they graduate *summa cum laude*.

At work you might be named the employee of the month and receive access to the best parking space for a few weeks. On a broader level our culture emphasizes national awards like the Pulitzer Prize, which recognizes outstanding writing, and the Nobel Prizes, which recognize outstanding achievements in several different fields.

What awards and accolades are you most proud of receiving?

What award or accolade do you hope to receive one day?

So what about the kingdom of God? Is there a way to receive a gold star from Jesus or to graduate summa cum laude from our lives here on earth? Is there a specific accolade we should be shooting for as we seek to love and serve God?

The answer to those questions can be found in Jesus' parable of the talents from Matthew 25:

*He who had received the five talents came forward, bringing five talents more, saying, "Master, you delivered to me five talents; here I have made five talents more." His master said to him, "Well done, good and **faithful** servant. You have been faithful over a little; I will set you over much. Enter into the joy of your master." Matthew 25:20-21, emphasis added*

As servants of God, we should all aspire to faithfulness.

WE MUST SERVE FAITHFULLY

The concept of faithfulness can mean different things to different people, so let's start with a few dictionary definitions:

Faithful: strict or thorough in the performance of duty; ... true to one's word, promises, vows, etc.; steady in allegiance or affection; loyal; constant.[1]

Here's my summary definition of *faithfulness: constant in the performance of duty.* In the context of serving God, people are faithful when they don't give up or shut down; they just keep on doing what God's called them to do.

> **What ideas or images come to mind when you hear the word *faithful*?**

> **Whom do you know who demonstrates faithfulness in service to God and others?**

The New Testament has a lot to say about faithfulness in serving God, including these words by the apostle Paul:

This is how one should regard us, as servants of Christ and stewards of the mysteries of God. Moreover, it is required of stewards that they be found faithful.
1 Corinthians 4:1-2

That word *stewards,* by the way, is just another way of referring to our role as followers of Jesus. The idea of stewardship is that everything belongs to God, and He's entrusted us with resources to use in His kingdom. So we're stewards of the gospel message entrusted to us. That's why Jesus emphasized the importance of faithfulness when it comes to using our money and other resources in service to God:

One who is faithful in a very little is also faithful in much, and one who is dishonest in a very little is also dishonest in much. If then you have not been faithful in the unrighteous wealth, who will entrust to you the true riches? And if you have not been faithful in that which is another's, who will give you that which is your own? Luke 16:10-12

What would it look like for Christians to be "dishonest" (v. 10) with the resources they've been given?

When have you had the opportunity to be faithful with "a very little" (v. 10)? What happened?

To serve God means to give of ourselves and of our resources to advance His kingdom. And only by serving faithfully—by remaining constant in the performance of our duty—can we make the kind of impact God intends in our communities and in the world.

OVERCOMING OBSTACLES TO FAITHFUL SERVICE

Unfortunately, several obstacles frequently prevent followers of Jesus from being faithful in their service. I want to look at two specific obstacles that I believe are extremely destructive in today's culture.

Busyness. Busyness is a devastating plague of modern society. It's so easy for us to surround ourselves with more responsibilities at work, more projects around the house, more hobbies, more TV shows, more obligations until, feeling completely overwhelmed, we decide we have no time to fulfill our primary role as a servant of God.

As a pastor, I've heard this many times over the years. "Our plates are just a little too full to serve in that ministry right now." "I think that's a great opportunity for ministry, but I'm overcommitted as it is." "We'd love to help, but we've already got a full schedule."

Busyness is a poison that slowly and steadily kills our ability to serve God and others. But living as an authentic follower of Christ means serving faithfully even when your schedule is full.

On a scale of 1 to 10, how busy is your current schedule from week to week?

1	2	3	4	5	6	7	8	9	10
Not busy at all								Completely booked	

How do you usually set priorities and budget your time when you feel busy?

Quitting. The second obstacle to faithful Christian service is our cultural obsession with quitting when things get tough. We hear it from so many quarters. If something isn't making you happy, get rid of it. If you're not happy in your marriage, get a divorce. If you don't feel spiritually fed at your current church, find a new one. If your job isn't leading to fulfillment and success, quit and find a new one.

When we find ourselves in a difficult situation and we're tempted to quit—especially in ministry and service to God—we need to remember Jesus' example. In John 13, just before Jesus was betrayed by His friend and headed for the cross, we read these words:

Before the Feast of the Passover, when Jesus knew that his hour had come to depart out of this world to the Father, having loved his own who were in the world, he loved them to the end. John 13:1

Jesus loved us to the end. He was in the middle of the worst experience imaginable, and He knew He would have to go through it alone, deserted by His disciples. But He didn't quit. He kept going. Jesus persevered because of His love for us; we should persevere because of our love for Him.

In what ministry situations are you most tempted to quit?

What gifts has God given you to help you keep serving even in the middle of difficult circumstances?

Our service to God and others is most effective when we're faithful to do what we've been called to do—when we don't ditch our responsibilities because we're busy with other stuff and when we refuse to quit even when things get tough. That's what it means to live as authentic servants of Christ, our Master.

DAY 4

HOW TO BE THE GREATEST SERVANT

We've been exploring the spiritual discipline of service this week. As followers of Jesus, we're called to invest ourselves and our resources in kingdom service, demonstrating love for others (the Great Commandment) and helping them grow as disciples of Jesus Christ (the Great Commission). That's what it means to live as servants in God's kingdom.

But as we carry out our role as servants, we must not expect God to serve us before we've completed our tasks in service to Him; we must not expect to receive an immediate reward or return for the work we do. Rather, we must view our service as our natural response and proper obligation to Jesus Christ.

Yesterday we learned that our primary aspiration in serving God is to be faithful in our service—to be constant in the performance of our duties in His kingdom. We also saw that a number of obstacles can prevent us from serving faithfully, including the rampant busyness of our culture and the modern temptation to quit when things get hard.

> How has your understanding of what it means to serve God and others changed through this week's study?

> What are your current goals for living as a servant in God's kingdom?

Today we're going to examine another principle from John 13, and I want to make sure we understand the context of this passage. Jesus' three years of public ministry were coming to an end. All of the crowds were gone. The many miracles were done. Jesus was alone with His disciples for His last meal before going to the cross.

If you were in Jesus' place, how would you make the most of your time to prepare the disciples for the road ahead? Would you give another landmark sermon? Maybe a miracle to really drive home your authority? Would you draw up strategies for launching the church and dealing with all of the struggles later recorded in the Book of Acts?

None of those things happened, of course. Instead, Jesus did something truly radical.

SOMETIMES WE NEED TO SERVE IN SILENCE

Look at John 13:3-5:

Jesus, knowing that the Father had given all things into his hands, and that he had come from God and was going back to God, rose from supper. He laid aside his outer garments, and taking a towel, tied it around his waist. Then he poured water into a basin and began to wash the disciples' feet and to wipe them with the towel that was wrapped around him.

What emotions do you experience when you read these verses?

How do these verses contribute to your understanding of what it means to serve God and others?

Jesus and His disciples would have been eating in an upper room with a rough wooden floor and thin mats for seating. The men may have kicked off their sandals at the door, but their feet would have been caked with whatever they'd walked through during their trip from Bethany to Jerusalem.

In those days it was customary for a servant, a hired person—*not* the host or the other guests—to take off the participants' sandals and wash their feet in preparation for the meal. That detail, however, had been overlooked in this situation. Jesus decided to transform that oversight into a teachable moment for the ages. And notice that He did so without saying a word.

How do you typically respond when you're exposed to silence?

Let's be honest: there are moments in life when the time for talking is done—when there aren't any words to say. There are moments when advice, platitudes, and clichés hurt a lot more than they help. And often the best choice we can make in those moments is simply to shut up and serve.

WE MUST ALWAYS SERVE WITH HUMILITY

Jesus' silent action of washing His disciples' feet must have been shocking for the men who experienced it. But it was probably a convicting experience for the disciples as well, because they spent time that evening arguing over which of them was the greatest. We know that because of the additional context provided in Luke 22: "A dispute also arose among them, as to which of them was to be regarded as the greatest" (v. 24).

Can you imagine the scene? While Jesus was preparing to go to the cross, the disciples were literally arguing—having a dispute—over which one of them deserved the gold star for disciple of the month. And in the middle of their raised voices and trash talking, Jesus silently got up, took off His outer clothes, and began washing their feet.

In the midst of worldly bravado, Jesus was a perfect picture of humility.

What ideas or images come to mind when you hear the word *humility*?

Whom among your friends and family would you characterize as humble?

After a brief interlude in which Peter put his foot in his mouth yet again, Jesus helped the disciples debrief the example He'd given them of humble service:

When he had washed their feet and put on his outer garments and resumed his place, he said to them, "Do you understand what I have done to you? You call me Teacher and Lord, and you are right, for so I am. If I then, your Lord and Teacher, have washed your feet, you also ought to ..." John 13:12-14

Wouldn't it have made sense for Jesus to say, "You also ought to wash My feet"? It would have made sense for Jesus to say, "I've washed your feet so that you'll know the right way to treat Me, your Master." That's probably what the disciples expected Him to say. And they were probably ready to argue over who got to be first at washing Jesus' feet!

But Jesus didn't say they should wash His feet. He said something much more revolutionary:

If I then, your Lord and Teacher, have washed your feet, you also ought to **wash one another's feet.** *For I have given you an example, that you also should do just as I have done to you. Truly, truly, I say to you, a servant is not greater than his master, nor is a messenger greater than the one who sent him.* John 13:14-16, emphasis added

What can we learn from these verses about the spiritual discipline of service?

Jesus was intentionally setting a standard for His disciples. He gave an example of humble service to be followed by the disciples in the room and by His followers who came later in history, including you and me.

Because we're His followers, Jesus expects us to serve Him and the people around us. And He's made it clear that we should serve with humility.

What steps can you take this week to focus on remaining humble as you serve and minister for Christ?

The discipline of service isn't hard to figure out. Jesus showed us how to do it. You've been blessed by the service of others, and you've probably had experience serving in God's kingdom now and then. But we'll become authentic servants of Christ only when we humbly embrace our daily, lifelong role as a servant in the house of our Master.

DAY 5

SERVICE AND YOU

Let me tell you about Howard. He and his wife have been coming to Harvest Bible Chapel for almost 20 years. Most people in our church don't know him, and those who do just know him as Howard. He's one of the ever-present guys who make the nuts, bolts, doorways, and bathrooms function the way they're supposed to in a building designed for thousands of people.

I often see Howard outside in the parking lot of our church as well. He helps people in the summer when it's boiling hot, and he helps people in the winter when it's bone-chilling cold. He's a faithful servant of Jesus Christ, and he loves doing whatever he can to serve others because he's so aware of what Christ has done for him.

> Whom do you consider a Howard in your church? Why?

> How has your life been influenced by the dedicated service of other Christians?

I'd like to encourage the Howards who might be reading this to keep up the good servant work. Let me urge you to keep doing what you're doing even if no one recognizes you or thanks you. Keep going because you're not really serving the people in the church. You're serving the Lord.

Is it hard sometimes? Do you want to quit sometimes? Yes, and that's natural. But authentic faith will help you push through the hardship and serve your Master well.

> How would you like others to describe you as a servant of Christ? Record three examples of what you hope others will say about you one day.

> 1.

> 2.

> 3.

I'd like to finish this week's study by giving you a chance to evaluate your current efforts to serve God and others in light of the principles we've explored this week. I'd also like you to consider other opportunities to make a difference for God's kingdom through authentic, humble service.

SERVICE EVALUATION

Use the following questions to gain a better understanding of your current motivations and expectations in serving God.

DO YOU EXPECT GOD TO SERVE YOU BEFORE YOU'VE SERVED HIM?

The Bible tells us that we "were bought with a price" (1 Cor. 6:20). That means God owns us. He's the Master, and we're servants in His house. So why do we often expect Him to get up from His table and serve us instead of the other way around?

Is it common or uncommon for you to feel that God owes you something?

When you pray, what percentage of your conversations with God revolve around things you want Him to do for you?

On a scale of 1 to 10, how often do you expect God to serve you, even though you haven't finished serving Him?

1	2	3	4	5	6	7	8	9	10
Almost never								All the time	

DO YOU EXPECT AN IMMEDIATE RETURN FOR YOUR SERVICE?

We should never serve God and others with the expectation that God will immediately bless and reward us because of that service. That's not how it works in the kingdom. Instead, our reward will come when we see Jesus face-to-face and hear Him say, "Well done, good and faithful servant" (Matt. 25:23).

Is it common or uncommon for you to feel angry with God for failing to meet your expectations?

When you pray, how often do you remind God of the ways you've served Him?

On a scale of 1 to 10, how likely are you to expect an immediate reward when you serve God and others?

1	2	3	4	5	6	7	8	9	10
Not likely									Very likely

DO YOU SEE SERVICE AS YOUR OBLIGATION TO JESUS?

Showing love to God and others through generosity and acts of service isn't an optional activity for followers of Jesus; it's a command. We have a duty to perform as Christians, and it includes the discipline of service.

Would you describe your efforts in ministry as consistent or inconsistent?

What are your primary motivations for participating in ministry?

On a scale of 1 to 10, how committed are you to serving Jesus Christ as an obligation rather than an option?

1	2	3	4	5	6	7	8	9	10
Not committed								Highly committed	

DO YOU SERVE FAITHFULLY?

To serve in a faithful way means we're constant in performing our duty to love God and minister to others. We don't give up or quit even when we don't feel like serving and even when circumstances become difficult.

To what degree is your willingness to serve affected by the busyness of your schedule?

How often have you quit your commitment to serve?

On a scale of 1 to 10, how would you rate yourself as a faithful servant of Christ?

1	2	3	4	5	6	7	8	9	10

Not faithful   Very faithful

FUTURE SERVICE

Use these final questions to discover potential opportunities for service in the future.

What are some of the primary problems or areas of need in your church?

What are some of the primary problems or areas of need in your community and on your street?

What are the main gifts, talents, and resources with which you've been blessed? Record as many as you can think of.

How can you use those gifts, talents, and resources to address or improve some of the problem areas you listed?

When it comes to living as an authentic follower of Jesus, there's no substitute for the discipline of service. It vividly demonstrates the love of Christ, providing rich opportunities to introduce people to Him. So go out this week, fulfill your obligation as a servant in God's house, and remember how glorious it will be one day to hear the words "Well done, good and faithful servant. … Enter into the joy of your master" (Matt. 25:21).

1. "Faithfulness," Dictionary.com [online, cited 15 April 2013]. Available from the Internet: http://dictionary.reference.com.

THE DISCIPLINE OF WORSHIP

WELCOME BACK TO THIS GROUP DISCUSSION OF
AUTHENTIC: DEVELOPING THE DISCIPLINES OF A SINCERE FAITH.

The previous session's application activity challenged you to have a conversation with an individual who's faithfully served God in your community.

- What did you enjoy most about that conversation?

- What surprised you about that conversation?

Describe what you liked best about the lessons in week 6. What questions do you have?

How will you fulfill your obligation to serve God in the coming weeks?

What ideas or images come to mind when you hear the word *worship?*

To prepare for the DVD segment, read aloud the following verses.

> *The heavens declare the glory of God,*
> *and the sky above proclaims his handiwork.*
> *Day to day pours out speech,*
> *and night to night reveals knowledge.*
> *There is no speech, nor are there words,*
> *whose voice is not heard.*
> *Psalm 19:1-3*

WATCH

COMPLETE THE VIEWER GUIDE BELOW AS YOU WATCH DVD SESSION 7.

Worship is the most powerful, _joy - producing_, _hope - sustaining_, _life - altering_ thing we do.

When worship is directed to an unworthy person or an unworthy object, we call it _idolatry_.

THE DISCIPLINE OF WORSHIP

Worship is _powerful_.

To fail at _worship_ is the greatest human failure of which we are capable because it _Robs_ us of what we were created by God to experience.

Worship: to fall or _prostrate_ yourself before someone on the ground

Worship is the _conscious_, direct, specific adoration of someone or something greater than ourselves.

Worship is _joy - producing_.

Worship is _life - altering_.

Worship is _hope - sustaining_.

In order to see the Lord fill what is empty in me, quench what is thirsty in me, satisfy what is hungry in my soul, I have to be _exposed_ for who I really am.

Growing in Worship

Avoid _debate_.

Worship isn't a mountain issue; it's a _motive_ issue.
Worship isn't a where thing; it's a _How_ thing.
Worship isn't a place; it's a _pattern_.

Start with _Salvation_. You can't worship a God you don't _Know_.

We should never get tired of our _story_.

God will not let go of _you_.

Enter in _fully_.

Worship in Spirit and Truth

1. _Vertical_
2. _Simple_
3. _Emotive_
4. _physical_

Focus on _Jesus Christ_.

DISCUSS THE DVD SEGMENT WITH YOUR GROUP, USING THE QUESTIONS BELOW.

What did you like best about James's teaching?

Respond to James's primary point in the message: "Worship is the most powerful, joy-producing, hope-sustaining, life-altering thing we do."

How have you seen idolatry reflected in today's society?

How have you seen idolatry reflected in your life?

What emotions do you experience in typical moments of corporate worship? What about in personal worship?

What would you like to experience when you practice the discipline of worship?

How can we as a group support and encourage one another in our efforts to practice the discipline of worship?

Application. Sit together as a group during the next corporate worship gathering at your church. When the service is over, briefly gather as a group to discuss what you experienced, what helped you connect with God, and how you hope to continue growing as a worshiper of God.

This week's Scripture memory. John 4:24

God is spirit, and those who worship him must worship in spirit and truth.

Assignment. Read week 7 and complete the activities to conclude this study.

Video sessions available for purchase
at *www.lifeway.com/authentic*

DISCOVERING TRUE WORSHIP

One of my earliest and most powerful experiences with the authentic practice of worship came in the the early 1980s on a visit to the original Calvary Chapel in Costa Mesa, California. As soon as I arrived, I felt a sense of purpose in the gathering. There was expectation in the air. I guessed at the time that the people were just excited about being together; now I realize I was among people who were actually anticipating meeting with God!

During the first 45 minutes of the worship service, I felt myself powerfully drawn into an atmosphere where people were not just singing about God but *to God*. They were singing from their spirits to God. They were creating new music that echoed Bible themes and directing them back to God—love songs to the Lord.

The impact on me was physical, emotional, and awesome. I wept as I realized I was in God's presence.

Not only was the direction of the singing new to me, but I had also never been in a setting where the glory of God was so manifest among His people. It was intimate; genuine; personal; and, as I now describe it, vertical. In our praise and worship, God had come down to be among us!

What I've learned since that first experience is that there's power in Spirit-filled worship. Something transformational happens when God's people come together in unity of purpose and lift our hearts toward heaven in a vertical expression of worship. When that happens, God's glory comes down among us.

This is why the discipline of worship energizes all of the other spiritual disciplines we've studied. In fact, increasingly vibrant worship is the reason we undertake other disciplines in the first place. If our spiritual practices don't lead us to a heightened, humbling sense of God's presence and create an overwhelming hunger to experience Him, then they haven't accomplished their intended purpose in our lives as disciples of Christ.

DAY 1

UNDERSTANDING WORSHIP

You may be surprised to hear it, but our culture is very good at the practice of worship. Think of the way we treat prominent Hollywood actors and actresses. Certain magazines and TV shows are entirely dedicated to the minute details of their lives, and people work religiously to keep track of every rumor and morsel of gossip from that world.

Similarly, many people in modern society adore professional athletes and sports teams. Again, entire networks on television and the Internet keep us informed 24 hours a day about scores, statistics, and upcoming games. We spend billions of dollars each year to watch games in person, shout praises to our favorite athletes, and decorate our homes— not to mention our backs—with their names and logos.

Yes, we know a lot about worship in today's world. Unfortunately, we don't have a great understanding of the proper methods and the vital importance of worshiping *God*. That makes us living subjects of Paul's warning in the Book of Romans:

God gave them up in the lusts of their hearts to impurity, to the dishonoring of their bodies among themselves, because they exchanged the truth about God for a lie and worshiped and served the creature rather than the Creator, who is blessed forever! Romans 1:24-25

What ideas or images come to mind when you hear the word *worship*?

Why is it tempting for us to worship and serve the creature rather than the Creator?

Throughout this study we've explored a number of spiritual disciplines—practices and principles we can put into action to help us grow in sincere faith. But the discipline of worship trumps everything else we've talked about so far. Indeed, worship is far and away the most important thing you and I can do in this life. In fact, it's the primary reason you and I were created in the first place.

Read the following passages of Scripture and record what they teach about our main purpose of worshiping and glorifying God.

> ROMANS 11:36

> 1 CORINTHIANS 6:19-20

> REVELATION 4:11

Worship is the most important practice we'll explore in this study. So let's make sure we understand what it really means to worship God.

DEFINITIONS

All sorts of ideas may come into your head when you hear the term *worship*. In Scripture many words for *worship* are translated *praise or adore, magnify, rejoice,* or *give thanks.* All of these are components or aspects of worship. Literally every page of the Bible contains the idea of worshiping God. We were created and saved so that we would be "to the praise of His glory" (Eph. 1:12). We were made to worship.

The word most often translated *worship* in the Old Testament literally means *to bow before.* It conveys the idea of pressing your forehead all the way down to the ground. The term expresses extreme humility and recognition of the infinite superiority of the One worshiped.

In the New Testament two Greek words are translated *worship.* One of them, *proskuneo,* means *to kiss toward* or *to kiss the hand.* It conveys the idea of adoration. The other word, *latreuo,* means *to give or to pay homage* or *to ascribe worth or value.*

Taking all that into account, I've come up with a condensed definition of *worship* for followers of Jesus Christ today. True worship is the conscious, direct, specific adoration of God. That's authentic worship.

What's your initial reaction to the previous definition of *worship*?

What kinds of activities would qualify as true worship, according to that definition?

This kind of true worship was the first thing God had in mind when He gave Moses the Ten Commandments on Mount Sinai:

You shall have no other gods before me. You shall not make for yourself a carved image, or any likeness of anything that is in heaven above, or that is in the earth beneath, or that is in the water under the earth. You shall not bow down to them or serve them, for I the LORD your God am a jealous God. Exodus 20:3-5

What's your reaction to the idea that the Lord is a jealous God (see v. 5)?

Conscious, direct, specific adoration isn't something we throw around lightly from one object to the next. That kind of worship is reserved only for God.

That's why idolatry is the worst of all possible sins. If worship is the highest and most powerful human experience, then the worst thing we can do is direct our adoration toward something that's unworthy of our worship—which is everything in the universe except God. Idolatry is wrong not only because it insults God but also because it insulates our hearts from the kind of delight and purpose we were created to experience.

Unfortunately, our culture specializes in idolatry. We love worshiping all kinds of people, places, activities, and ideas—all of which are unworthy of our adoration. This has even led to several misconceptions about worship.

MISCONCEPTIONS

Misconception 1: We can worship through our everyday experiences. We may say things like "I can worship God in the way I fill out an expense report." "I can worship God in the way I cook a meal for my family." "I can worship God by shopping a certain way."

Wrong! Worshiping the Creator of the universe isn't an accessory we can tag on to other activities like a pair of earrings. Yes, we can approach some parts of our lives in a way that's *worshipful*, but that's not worship. Remember our definition: authentic worship is the conscious, direct, specific adoration of God. That doesn't happen on a whim.

What's your reaction to the previous statements?

What are the benefits of approaching different activities in a way that's worshipful?

How are these activities different from an intentional, specific time of true worship?

Misconception 2: We can worship one day a week. We think we can show up for church in order to be seen and get an A for attendance, although our hearts are actually far from God. In other words, we act a certain way on Sunday, and then we act a completely different way on Monday. That's hypocrisy.

Misconception 3: We can keep worship on the surface. We come to church or a small group and do all the things we're supposed to—all the things we've been doing for decades, in some cases—but we have no heart for it. We don't realize we've come into the presence of Most Holy God. This is the kind of worship that just goes through the motions.

Here's the problem with all of these misconceptions about worship: God always looks into our hearts when we come before Him:

> *Every way of a man is right in his own eyes,*
> *but the Lord weighs the heart. Proverbs 21:2*

In what situations do you find yourself going through the motions of worship?

How have you recently experienced authentic worship?

As followers of Jesus, we have an incredible opportunity to worship the Creator and Sustainer of the universe. Let's take advantage of that privilege and commit to worship as the conscious, direct, specific adoration of our God.

DAY 2

THE PRACTICE OF WORSHIP

Yesterday we defined true worship as the conscious, direct, specific adoration of God. Now it's time to focus on action. Worship is a spiritual discipline, which means it's ultimately something we *do*—something that requires intentionality and movement. We need to go beyond thinking about worship and intellectually agreeing that worship is important. We need to practice worship in our lives and in our churches.

Thankfully, Jesus gave us a very useful framework for thinking about worship in practical terms. He delivered this framework after being asked by a scribe to identify the most important commandment:

Jesus answered, "The most important is, 'Hear, O Israel: The Lord our God, the Lord is one. And you shall love the Lord your God with all your heart and with all your soul and with all your mind and with all your strength.'" Mark 12:29-30

What emotions do you experience when you read these verses? Why?

How do you specifically and intentionally "love the Lord your God" (v. 30) in your everyday life?

Because authentic worship is one of the most important things we do to express our love for God, Jesus' words in these verses give us a structure for the active practice of worship. So let's go deeper and look at what it means to worship God with our minds, our heart and soul, and our strength.

THOUGHTFUL WORSHIP

As followers of Jesus, we have an opportunity and an obligation to worship God with our minds. And I'm not talking about a sliver of our intellectual capacity. I'm not talking about reading a blog post every now and then or spending five minutes a week using our brains to think thoughts toward God while we sing.

No. The Bible says, "You shall love the Lord your God with ... *all* your mind" (v. 30, emphasis added). You and I are called to use every ounce of brainpower we can muster in our efforts to worship God. God wants us to think great thoughts about Him.

What that means practically is that we can greatly expand our capacity to worship by studying God's Word—by digging deep into the Bible on a regular, consistent basis. We can enhance our ability to understand and respond to God's Word by memorizing prayers, psalms, and other passages of Scripture.

We can also expand our capacity to worship by studying the lives of those who've gone before us and by reading great writing on worship. That may include reading biographies, but it can also be as simple as reading hymns and bathing ourselves in the time-tested expressions of worship that have been passed down through the centuries.

In what ways do you currently worship God with your mind and thoughts?

What are some additional practices with which you can experiment this week during your times of worship?

Worshiping God with our minds applies on a congregational level as well. At the church where I serve as the pastor, we try hard to avoid singing meaningless songs or leading our people through superficial worship experiences.

For example, we've rejected worship songs that frame our relationship with Jesus in terms of romantic love. Given our culture's obsession with twisting the meaning and application of romance, such songs can cause a lot of damage and confusion on an intellectual level, hindering us from worshiping God with all our minds.

What are some song lyrics that help you worship God with your mind? Record three examples.

1.

2.

3.

To participate in authentic worship means to love God with all your mind.

EMOTIVE WORSHIP

To participate in authentic worship also means to "love the Lord your God with all your heart and with all your soul" (v. 30). The combination of worshiping God with our hearts and souls is a necessary component of authentic worship.

To understand this emotional aspect of worship and to understand how it relates to the thoughtful worship we just examined, we need to look at Jesus' conversation with the Samaritan woman in John 4. We've already reviewed their interaction in light of the discipline of fasting, but Jesus' teaching in this passage is also vital for understanding how to worship God.

> Read John 4:7-26. How do these verses contribute to your understanding of worship?

After Jesus gently but directly exposed the Samaritan woman's sinfulness and need for forgiveness (see vv. 16-18), she changed the subject by asking a question about worship: should people focus on a specific location (Mount Zion or Mount Gerizim) when they approach God? She had a cultural misunderstanding of what it means to worship God.

Jesus corrected her misunderstanding in verses 21-22, but He didn't stop there. Look at what He said next:

The hour is coming, and is now here, when the true worshipers will worship the Father in spirit and truth, for the Father is seeking such people to worship him. God is spirit, and those who worship him must worship in spirit and truth (vv. 23-24).

If we want to experience authentic worship, if we want to be "true worshipers" (v. 23), we must approach God in two ways: in spirit and truth (see v. 24). Those are the primary elements of authentic worship. We addressed the "in truth" part in our discussion of thoughtful worship; we worship in truth by worshiping God with all our minds.

To worship God in spirit means to worship Him with all our hearts and all our souls. It means we feel something when we come before God in worship. It means we worship in a way that engages our feelings, our emotions, our inner selves, and our spirits.

That's what John Piper was talking about when he wrote these words:

Without the engagement of the heart, we do not really worship. The engagement of the heart in worship is the coming alive of the feelings and emotions and affections of the heart. Where feelings for God are dead, worship is dead.[1]

What helps you connect with God on an emotional level?

Read the following passages of Scripture and record the feelings and emotions communicated in each expression of worship.

PSALM 42:1-5

PSALM 51:1-12

PSALM 95:1-5

If we want to practice the discipline of worship, we must be willing to engage with God not just intellectually but also emotionally.

STRONG WORSHIP

Authentic worship involves your mind, your heart, and your soul, but there's one more ingredient Jesus highlighted in Mark 12. You're to worship God "with all your strength" (v. 30). There's a physical element in the practice of worship.

Scripture has a lot to say about engaging our bodies in the practice of worship. Psalm 47:1 says:

Clap your hands, all peoples!
Shout to God with loud songs of joy!

Do you feel the strength in those words? The physicality? Ezra 3:11 says the people of Israel "sang responsively" after laying the foundations for the temple. They "shouted with a great shout when they praised the LORD." Do you feel the volume in those words?

How would you feel about shouting or clapping your hands during a worship service?

In what circumstances do you feel most free to worship God loudly and with strength?

The Bible also connects worship and physical posture. Recall that the word translated *worship* in the Old Testament literally means *to press your forehead to the ground*. Paul wrote, "I desire then that in every place the men should pray, lifting holy hands without anger or quarreling" (1 Tim. 2:8). David became so emotionally caught up during a time of worship that he "danced before the LORD with all his might" (2 Sam. 6:14).

How do you currently use your body to engage in or enhance the practice of worship?

We're all made different. Some people are louder than others; some people have more rhythm than others. So I'm not saying everyone has to worship according to a certain style. But all of us should max ourselves out when we come before the Creator of the universe. We should worship Him with *all* our minds, *all* our hearts and souls, and *all* our strength—because He's worthy of *all* our praise.

THE IMPACT OF WORSHIP

Have you ever been skydiving? Bungee jumping? Have you ever done something foolish or dangerous simply because you wanted to experience the sensations that come with doing something foolish or dangerous?

There's nothing innately immoral or sinful about skydiving or other extreme hobbies. I'm not against these kinds of activities. I'm also not averse to more tame methods of seeking excitement, such as riding a motorcycle, hiking through mountain trails, surfing, scuba diving, and so on. But I think it's important for us to examine the inner motivations that cause us to pursue such practices. What are we *really* looking for? What are we trying to achieve?

What hobby or activity do you find exciting or exhilarating?

What motivates you to pursue it?

I firmly believe that if we as followers of Jesus had a better understanding of worship, we wouldn't rely so much on thrills and danger to quench our desire for excitement. If we had more experiences with authentic worship—all our minds, all our hearts and souls, and all our strength—we'd find more than enough exhilaration in our everyday lives.

In short, authentic worship is the most powerful, joy-producing, hope-sustaining, life-altering thing we can experience as human beings. Let's take a look at some of the reasons.

WORSHIP BRINGS GOD'S PRESENCE

A primary reason authentic worship is such a powerful, life-altering experience is that it brings us into the presence of God. That's why Psalm 22:3 says:

> *You are holy,*
> *enthroned on the praises of Israel.*

That word *enthroned,* used a thousand times in the Old Testament, means *the place where someone resides or dwells*—where someone sits. The King James Version says God inhabits the praises of His people. In other words, God sits down and settles into the praises of His people. He's comfortable there.

Picture a throne room where all of God's people are standing around Him. Imagine coming into the room and seeing lots of people standing except for one person in the center, who's seated. You'd think, *Whoa, that person must be very important. Everyone's standing in that person's honor.* That's the picture of God being enthroned on the praises of His people. Matthew 18 expresses a similar idea:

If two of you agree on earth about anything they ask, it will be done for them by my Father in heaven. For where two or three are gathered in my name, there am I among them (vv. 19-20).

When have you felt connected with God while gathered with other believers?

Something special happens when we get together for authentic worship. God is enthroned, and we experience His presence. Keep in mind, however, that though God is present, He isn't tame. He's the all-powerful Creator of the universe, which means the manifestation of His presence can often knock us out of our comfort zones.

That's what the people of Israel experienced when they met with God.

Read the following passages of Scripture and record what they communicate about the power of God's presence.

EXODUS 19:16-24

2 CHRONICLES 7:1-3

Authentic, Spirit-filled worship brings the presence of God. And when God shows up, some really big things can happen. Let's look at some of those.

WORSHIP BRINGS SALVATION

The apostle Paul wrote some interesting instructions to the church in Corinth that help us grasp the power of worship in our congregations. Here are the verses:

If, therefore, the whole church comes together and all speak in tongues, and outsiders or unbelievers enter, will they not say that you are out of your minds? But if all prophesy, and an unbeliever or outsider enters, he is convicted by all, he is called to account by all, the secrets of his heart are disclosed, and so, falling on his face, he will worship God and declare that God is really among you.
1 Corinthians 14:23-25

What ideas or images come to mind when you hear the phrase "speak in tongues" (v. 23)?

What ideas or images come to mind when you hear the word *prophecy*?

Speaking in tongues is a subject that creates a lot of debate in the church. The potential for confusion that Paul mentioned in verse 23—"Will they not say that you are out of your minds?"—is the reason we don't encourage the public demonstration of that gift at the church where I serve.

Prophesying is another matter. We typically think of prophecy as predicting the future, and there are certainly instances of that happening in the Scriptures, specifically by those God appointed as prophets. But today the idea of prophesying means believers exhort, sing, and speak about the truth God has spoken in His Word. Prophecy is always based on Scripture—on what God has revealed and made known.

So imagine a church where God's Word is so respected and elevated that all of our conversations, preaching, and singing focuses on what God says. Imagine a worship experience in which believers consciously and specifically agree with God's Word and express their adoration to Him.

According to Paul, unbelievers who enter that kind of atmosphere will be convicted of their sin; recognize the presence of God; and fall on their faces to repent, receive His salvation, and worship Him.

When have you experienced God's presence during a time of worship?

When have you been convicted of your sin while worshiping God?

WORSHIP BRINGS HEALING

I'm convinced that authentic, Spirit-filled worship is the most powerful, joy-producing, hope-sustaining, life-altering thing we can experience as human beings. Worship brings us into God's presence. Worship brings salvation to those who need it. And finally, what could be more hope-sustaining than the knowledge that authentic worship brings healing to our lives? Jeremiah 17:14 says:

> Heal me, O LORD, and I shall healed;
> save me, and I shall be saved,
> for you are my praise.

This verse emphasizes that we must trust God for healing and restoration each day, just as we trust Him for our eternal salvation. We can't do anything to demand or earn those gifts. But what we *can* do each day is to praise Him!

I believe God heals people in many ways today, including miracles. We've seen people healed in our church, but it's always happened when those people first came to a place of authentic worship.

In what areas of your life and body do you currently need healing?

Have these areas of need caused you to pull away from God or draw nearer to Him? Explain.

Those who have sickness in their bodies often come to a place where they can present themselves to God and say, "My life belongs to You, Lord. Do whatever pleases You, because You are everything to me." That kind of surrender to God is the essence of authentic worship. The closer you come to Him and His presence, the closer you've come to the place of ultimate healing.

HOW TO GROW IN WORSHIP

I've been known to play a little golf from time to time. I don't get on the course as often as I'd like, partly because of my busy schedule and partly because of the weather (there's no such thing as winter golf where I live in Chicago). But when I get the chance to play 9 or 18 holes, I almost always enjoy the experience.

But what if I decided to become serious about the game of golf? I'd have to follow several steps to improve my golf game. For example, I'd have to start working with a swing coach. I'd probably have to join a local golf club and start playing every week, not to mention spending time on the driving range every other day or so. I'd also need to purchase new clubs and other equipment. If I committed to those steps and followed through, I could reasonably expect to improve my skills as a golfer.

In the same way I can follow a certain path to improve at golf, we can follow a few specific steps to grow and mature as worshipers of God. In fact, we can look again at John 4—Jesus' primary teaching on worship—and follow four specific steps to grow in our practice of authentic worship.

1. AVOID DEBATE

Remember that Jesus began talking about worship because the Samaritan woman asked Him a question that was hotly contested between the Jews and the Samaritans:

The woman said to him, "Sir, I perceive that you are a prophet. Our fathers worshiped on this mountain, but you say that in Jerusalem is the place where people ought to worship." Jesus said to her, "Woman, believe me, the hour is coming when neither on this mountain nor in Jerusalem will you worship the Father. You worship what you do not know; we worship what we know, for salvation is from the Jews." John 4:19-22

Notice that Jesus deflected the woman's question and avoided a debate about the appropriate place to worship. He clarified the subject without jumping into the cultural battle between Jews and Samaritans. Worship isn't a mountain issue; it's a motive issue. Worship isn't a *where* thing; it's a *how* thing. Worship isn't a place; it's a pattern and a practice for all believers.

Some fights aren't worth having. Debates about worship devalue people. They devalue the principle. They derail progress. They diminish the Lord. That's why Jesus refused this debate. Instead, He chose to instruct the woman about what her soul really needed.

When have you caused damage to yourself and others by jumping into a fight over something that was ultimately unimportant?

When have you concluded that a fight wasn't worth having?

Here's the sad thing: even though Jesus refused to debate about worship, that's not what's going on in the church today. In fact, worship is one of the most hotly debated topics in modern church culture. We as Christians fight about hymns. We fight about choirs. We fight about musical instruments. We fight about volume in worship. We fight about specific songs and styles.

And it's more than fighting. People have left the church I pastor simply because they didn't like specific elements of our worship. Worse, over and over again we hear about entire congregations splitting because of disagreements about worship. This is a huge issue in the church.

What debates about worship, if any, are currently contested in your church?

On a scale of 1 to 10, how strong is your opinion about those debates?

1	2	3	4	5	6	7	8	9	10
Not strong									Very strong

Let's let go of these unncecessary debates. Let's take the passion and drive we're wasting on arguments and direct them instead to the adoration of our God through worship.

2. START WITH SALVATION

Look again at Jesus' words in John 4:22: "You worship what you do not know; we worship what we know, for salvation is from the Jews." If you want to have a worship relationship with God, you have to start with salvation. That's the only way. You can't worship a God you don't know. You can't worship a God you haven't personally experienced through a saving relationship.

This truth is vitally important because millions of people know *about* God, but they don't know God. They haven't experienced God. They can't say along with David, "Oh, taste and see that the LORD is good!" (Ps. 34:8). And these aren't just atheistic heathens who've rejected Christianity; many of these people come to our churches every week.

Salvation is turning from my sin and placing my faith in Jesus Christ for my forgiveness. Have you done that?

What's your story of how you became a follower of Jesus?

How has your life changed since that moment? How has your worship changed since that moment?

When Jesus taught about worship, He avoided the debates and fads of His day. Instead, He pointed the Samaritan woman toward her need for salvation so that she could become a true worshiper of God.

3. ENTER FULLY

I don't know of another passage in God's Word that's personally impacted me more than what Jesus said next. His words are vital to the practice of worship:

The hour is coming, and is now here, when the true worshipers will worship the Father in spirit and truth, for the Father is seeking such people to worship him. God is spirit, and those who worship him must worship in spirit and truth.
John 4:23-24

Look at that phrase "true worshipers" (v. 23). That's what God wants! That's what He's expecting of us: "The Father is seeking such people to worship him" (v. 23). God is looking for people like you and me who will fully enter the practice of authentic worship—people who will worship Him in spirit and in truth.

Do you consider yourself to be a true worshiper of God? Explain.

This is what we've been exploring all week. Authentic worship is the conscious, direct, specific adoration of God. We worship God by coming before Him with *all* our minds— that's worshiping Him in truth. We come before Him with *all* our hearts and souls. That's worshiping Him in spirit.

We've thoroughly covered these themes on an intellectual level, but they mean nothing if you don't practice them in your everyday life. You have to fully enter the discipline of authentic worship on a personal level. All of us have multiple opportunities each day to consciously praise and adore God through worship. Do you make the most of them?

How do you feel about your recent experiences with personal worship?

In what areas would you like to get better at personal worship?

It's also important for you to fully enter the discipline of worship on a corporate level. There's a reason congregations all over the world gather each week, and it's not just to hear a sermon. Worshiping together is a vital part of being the church. So do you allow yourself to be caught up in this worldwide expression of praise, or do you hold back? Do you worship God with everything you have, or do you go through the motions?

What would it look like for you to fully enter a corporate worship experience?

What obstacles commonly prevent you from doing so?

4. FOCUS ON JESUS CHRIST

Jesus concluded His conversation with the Samaritan woman and His teaching on worship by affirming His role as the One to whom our worship is due:

The woman said to him, "I know that Messiah is coming (he who is called Christ). When he comes, he will tell us all things." Jesus said to her, "I who speak to you am he." John 4:25-26

What ideas or images come to mind when you hear the word *Messiah*?

Those who know me personally understand that I'm busy. I'm hardworking. I'm strong. I'm aggressive. I move forward. Those traits are valued and promoted by today's culture. Yet all of those traits can also become barriers in my heart as a worshiper of God.

Jesus is the solution to that obstacle. He said, "Unless you turn and become like children, you will never enter the kingdom of heaven" (Matt. 18:3). I cling to those words because the only time I feel that I can let go of my strength and my drive to get things done is when I come before Him in worship. That's the only time I can allow myself to be a child in His arms.

Jesus also referred to Himself as "the good shepherd" (John 10:11), which was a reference to Isaiah 40:11:

> *He will tend his flock like a shepherd;*
> *he will gather the lambs in his arms;*
> *he will carry them in his bosom,*
> *and gently lead those that are with young.*

How have you experienced the ministry of the Good Shepherd in worship?

These words are a balm for so many of us in today's society who desperately long for a place to acknowledge our needs and weaknesses. Jesus is that place. When we focus on Him through worship, He takes us in His arms and allows us to depend on Him. He cares for us because He's indeed the Messiah—the One we've been waiting for all our lives.

DAY 5

WORSHIP AND YOU

We're going to wrap up this week with a worship experience so that you can practice the principles we've explored. Take a minute or so to prepare yourself through prayer and then follow the instructions below. This experience focuses on personal worship, but you can practice the principles in corporate times of worship as well.

WORSHIP WITH ALL YOUR MIND

This worship experience will focus on Psalm 19. Written by David, this psalm contains wonderful expressions of praise to God in addition to David's thoughts and reflections about God and himself. It's a great example of what it means to worship both in spirit and in truth.

Begin by reading Psalm 19 two or three times without rushing. Contemplate and savor the different expressions in the verses just as you'd savor a fine meal.

What are your initial impressions of these verses?

Which words and phrases catch your attention? Which do you enjoy and appreciate most?

Which words and phrases do you have a harder time understanding?

Now focus more closely on the first three verses. How does nature declare and reveal the glory of God?

What have you learned about God from interactions with the natural world?

What have you recently learned about God through the study of His Word?

Never be afraid to use your mind as a tool for worshiping God. He's the source of truth. He knows all things. He's revealed much of Himself to us through words and intellectual concepts. Therefore, you have a great opportunity to respond to Him with your intellect and understanding. That's worship.

WORSHIP WITH ALL YOUR HEART AND SOUL

Now bring your heart and soul into this worship experience. Don't be content with simply understanding the words of this passage. Work to respond on an emotional level. Allow yourself to feel something. Then express those feelings to God.

Read Psalm 19 again. What feelings and emotions are mentioned?

What feelings and emotions do you experience as you read the following?

VERSES 1-6

VERSES 7-11

VERSES 12-14

Look specifically at verses 9-10. How do you feel when you study God's Word? What emotions or attitudes do you usually experience?

What do you want to experience in your relationship with God? What do you desire from Him?

Take a moment to express those desires now. Write them in a journal or speak with God in prayer.

To be a true worshiper, you must worship God in spirit and in truth. You must allow yourself to feel something deeper than intellectual understanding, and you must make the effort to express your feelings and desires to God.

WORSHIP WITH ALL YOUR STRENGTH

Read Psalm 19 again but out loud this time. Use your vocal cords to express praise and honor to God. Also worship with your body by adopting the following postures as you read this psalm a final time.

• *Verses 1-6.* Raise your head and lift your hands as you read these verses out loud. Allow your body to respond to the words. For example, look to the sky when you read, "The sky above proclaims his handiwork" (v. 1).

• *Verses 7-11.* As you read these verses, lower yourself to your knees as a sign of respect for God's Word. Physically touch the body parts mentioned in these verses—heart and eyes—to show that you've offered yourself to God.

• *Verses 12-14.* Bow your head to the ground as you read these verses. Prostrate yourself as an expression of your inability to find forgiveness on your own and your desperate need for God to make you blameless (see v. 13).

What's your initial reaction to worshiping God with your body?

How can you include these and other physical elements in your regular practice of worship as a discipline?

I trust this tour of the spiritual disciplines of a sincere faith has been encouraging and motivating for you. I hope you've learned much, and I pray you'll continue learning as you grow and mature in your faith. Most importantly, however, I hope you'll move beyond the realm of *learning* and into the arena of *practicing* the disciplines, with the goal of becoming more like Jesus. For that reason I'll leave you with His words from John 13:17: "If you know these things, blessed are you if you do them."

1. John Piper, *Desiring God,* rev. ed. (Colorado Springs: Multnomah Books, 2003), 87–88.

A NEW MODEL FOR CHURCH
IS DESPERATELY NEEDED

This study will help adults in your church get beyond the human-centered, horizontal church to focus on seeking God's glory. Participants will explore the four pillars that are foundational and essential for any vertical church: unashamed adoration, unapologetic preaching, unafraid witness, and unceasing prayer. Only a vertical church can reveal a holy God who shows up in power, changing hearts and altering lives. To learn more, go to lifeway.com/verticalchurch, call 800.458.2772, or visit the LifeWay Christian Store serving you.

Scan with your smartphone or visit
lifeway.com/verticalchurch to watch the promo video.